Books are to be re
the last c

Ideas Galore

by Patrick Goodland

Scripture Union, 47 Marylebone Lane, London W1M 6AX

© Patrick Goodland 1974

First published 1974

ISBN 0 85421 458 5

Printed in Great Britain by
Unwin Brothers Limited
The Gresham Press Old Woking Surrey
A member of the Staples Printing Group.

Preface

IDEAS GALORE is the result of an active programme in a North London surburban church, and I have put together in this book a selection of material which we have found useful and practical in our own local situation.

The purpose of the book is to encourage groups, youth fellowships and those working among children by providing 'grist for the mill' for inclusion in their regular programmes.

Young people of all ages need variety, and in compiling this book I have specially had in mind smaller units, clubs and fellowships who depend for leadership on devoted people with heavy commitments. Willing horses expend much energy and need feeding, and the diet in this book, which is I hope both varied and easily digestible, may provide nourishment and stimulate experiment. Many of the items, of course, are capable of adaptation and variation to meet local needs and to make use of local initiative.

A number of the ideas have no traceable origin; some have been contributed by friends whose help I gladly acknowledge. If any acknowledgment has been omitted, I offer apologies and will gladly rectify matters in any subsequent edition.

Patrick Goodland

Contents

Chapter 1

Introduction

The Christian Church has often implied that recreation is a doubtful procedure, with the result that for many people 'church' meant a place of dullness and often drabness. This is probably a legacy from the Victorians, most of whom worked such long hours that they had little time to do anything else.

We have moved a long way from the life style of the Victorians. Mechanization and technology have led to shorter working hours. We now have an enormous leisure industry helping us to fill up our spare time, and Christians need to think out their attitudes to leisure and to leisure opportunities that were beyond the Victorians' wildest dreams.

But Christians have by no means always been negative. Many older people look back with gratitude on enterprising Sunday School programmes and annual church outings, and in fact the idea of Bank Holidays sprang from Christian concern for the welfare of the whole population. Leisure time was gradually won for working people as a result of Christian influence. Because they have acknowledged that this is God's world and that man has been created to enjoy it, enlightened Christians have been insistent that man should have time for social pursuits.

The forerunners of package holiday tours were often Christians. Their concern was for man's well-being, wholeness and physical health and not just for profit. We take a five-day week and annual holiday as a right today, but fifty years ago these were not the privilege of the majority. Much social reform, including holiday benefits, was pioneered and eventually established as a result of the Christian conscience influenced by Biblical teaching.

Christian love (*agape*) seeks the highest good and wholeness of man. It is a creative, positive quality that is active in stimulating a benevolent atmosphere (Matt. 5: 43–45), in which people can grow into physical and spiritual maturity.

We are social beings, interdependent. God places us in families, in communities and in countries. This is his creative order to accomplish his overall purpose. God's providential blessings are common to all men (Matt. 5: 45). They are freely given by God for the benefit of men. The greater spiritual gifts of salvation and eternal life are for those who will respond to Him in personal commitment (John 3). God does care for His creatures' wholeness in every area of experience; this is implicit in the great Christian word 'salvation'. Only in a living relationship with Him can we appreciate and enjoy life in its deepest sense.

If there is to be social development, then some shared activities are essential. The Christian ethic of concern for another's 'wholesomeness' is built on his understanding of the nature and purpose of God, seen and demonstrated in Jesus Christ. This is so different from much Greek philosophy which, in contrast to Hebrew understanding, was lamentably lacking in concern. In general terms, the Greeks saw the gods as remote and isolated, not really bothered about man. They reasoned that if a god was isolated and untouchable, man must try to be like him. There was an accepted kind of fatalism. If a man is poor, a slave working all hours of the day and night, don't you worry about him: the gods want it that way. God is not disturbed by their condition—it is a matter of indifference to him.

The gospel which Jesus taught and demonstrated is in distinct contrast and is one of total concern. God is deeply concerned about His world and is committed and involved in our humanity and our human situation (Matt. 25: 31–46. Luke 10: 29–37). The Christian follows in the footsteps of his Lord and is consequently in relationship with other people.

It is interesting to notice that Jesus was concerned about spiritual and physical wholeness. Often in his healing ministry the latter took precedence over the former. This was not in any sense because Jesus felt that the physical should have priority over the spiritual. He was simply indicating that until a person is whole physically, is relaxed and able to think reasonably and to participate in life, it is difficult for him to enter into spiritual fellowship. A Church cannot communicate without being a community. It is, therefore, imperative that this sense of friendship should find expression first within the living members of the Church. This will then have its own impact on society.

Jesus came into this world as a man sharing the life and enjoyment of the family, home and community. He participated in the fun and social enjoyment of the human race— the wedding feast, the banquet, wholesome jokes with the publicans and sinners; the infectious humour of the family were all part and parcel of his life. Humanly he was no 'pale-faced Galilean' but a full-blooded country youth who matured into manhood with a sincerity, grace and charm which were magnetically attractive.

There is today a renewed interest in the wonder of God's creation and of our true humanity. For many this has led to a desire to stimulate the sense of community, so often lacking in our world, and to create it within the Christian Church. Without knowing people on an informal basis it is very difficult to relax with them and really to know them. Some of the simple pleasures and recreative activities which are becoming part and parcel of our Christian communities, are providing a real stimulus to people to become truly whole.

The ministry of Christ and the Church is to the whole person. The creative pleasures, suggestions and ideas in this book are offered as a contribution to help people to grow together into maturity and to enjoy God-given life in the community of love.

Chapter 2

Ideas for Leadership

'Is a leader born or in some mystic way sent from heaven?' Neither, but some people have more of an aptitude and personality than others. A 'do-it-yourself' enthusiast may not be so quick or precise in the use of his tools as a craftsman; he can, however, by application, stickability and involvement do the job, and earn the praise at least of his petticoat foreman!

Leadership is at a premium in voluntary organizations, and the choice is often limited. There is no quick 'crash course' for would-be leaders, and no one has yet found an encyclopedia which will give the prospective leader all the answers.

You may be the only person available in your group or Church, especially in a small community. Don't underestimate your role; your contribution to the development and integration into society of numerous young people could be invaluable. If you are committed to this task, you are in royal company among the first division of God's army. Many a man and woman owes his present position and appreciation of true Christian values to the influence of some dedicated youth leader in former years. You don't have to attend many 'old boy' reunions to know the reality of that debt.

In this brief chapter, we share just a few ideas about the qualities of leadership which seem to be most necessary. If you have them all, beware! You may be the archangel Gabriel, so watch your halo. We have in mind lesser mortals learning their trade, jobbing craftsman rather than specialists.

Optimism born out of a positive attitude to life will enable a leader to go on in the wake of disappointment. He will see creative possibilities in a situation, or in a young person. His attitude will communicate to the boys or girls the fact that someone believes in them. They will sense that the impossible will be done immediately, while the miracle will take a little longer, that the future has purpose if the right pathway is followed.

16

Enthusiasm. There are plenty of kicks to be taken from the others when a player is in the front row of the scrum. If you can accept the blows of disappointment in the front row of youth leadership and come up still an enthusiast, you'll always be an asset to the first team. Enthusiasm stems from the knowledge that the job is worthwhile. The Christian leader has as his supreme motive the wholeness of youth, which includes the physical and the spiritual. Jack and Jill will not be enthusiastic about the Jesus life if the leader is apologetic and tentative. Enthusiasm for life as a treasure God has given will enable the many facets of the faith to shine in unobscured brightness. A newly-engaged girl will often allow her fingers to be numbed with the frost if she can display her newly-acquired ring—the symbol of belonging. The many facets of a leader's enthusiastic Christianity—his love for the Bible, for other Christians and Christian standards of behaviour, will be infectious. This will permeate the whole of his task in the games, discipline and visitation of homes.

Preparation. Someone once wrote that 'enthusiasm without something in the stomach is usually a very windy affair.' Wafflers are really no use with youth. But informed leadership which bears the mark of careful preparation, will usually command a hearing and ensure respect. The muddler, the 'inspiration on the spot merchant', is as likely to impress as a flea on an elephant's back. Strategy, efficiency, an eye to detail, are not only duties, but give pleasure as the programme unfolds.

Punctuality. An unpunctual leader is as desirable as a rat in the rice pudding—he may rush around and stir the glutinous mass but the end product will be useless. Activities are timed for a particular hour, so having made a contract with your members, you must keep your promises.

Humility. Leaders don't usually aspire to be models of fashion; they are usually like the works of the clock, self-effacing. We should dress suitably and convey by our personal appearance that we really do believe that cleanliness is next to godliness. One major role is that of example. Humbly we serve. Such is the psychology of teen-mindedness that hero-worship or at least example-worship invariably occurs.

Parent-group relationships are of tremendous value. A leader who knows home backgrounds and is at least on a nodding acquaintance with parents will usually have at least one faithful pair of allies.

Mediocrity and expediency are luxuries which are priced out of the budget in youth work. Dedication, humility and the sheer slog of learning the craft are the staple diet of success.

'There are creative opportunities in every situation.'

Chapter 3

Ideas for the Programme

1. Basic Principles

The success of most enterprises depends on planning. There are few geniuses who can really 'run' an evening, give a talk, entertain a bunch of young people, alone and impromptu. Careful planning encourages confidence and helps to develop potential leadership. Shared responsibility not only lightens a load but often leads to the discovery of latent talent. A representative committee should be the aim.

(1) Allow adequate time for careful planning, publicity, and the collection of any props or equipment which may need to be assembled.

(2) Have a minimum number of committee meetings. Ensure that members are given prior notice of the agenda. This encourages a thoughtful approach and should save time.

(3) Delegate responsibility, being careful not to overload the novice. The wise leader will encourage gradual development. This saves the youngsters from despair and guards against big-headedness.

(4) Evaluate your efforts, frankly and in a spirit of charity, at any 'post-mortem' session after a programme. Be prepared to debit some mistakes to the experience account of those who may have failed to fulfil their part adequately. Analyse why the more successful times were popular. This will help to improve similar efforts.

(5) Consider your budget carefully and work within it.

2. Planning a party or social

Think carefully about the purpose of your party. Is it to act as a bridge for friendship? to promote a special event or organization? or to give people an opportunity to thaw?

Decide on the form, or the theme, it is to take. (See 'Themes' for parties.) Times, seasons, special times of celebration will often have a bearing on the kind of event to be planned. Appoint an M.C., caterer, decorator and other helpers. All decorations should be in place and safely secured well before starting time.

Draw up a suggested programme, timing each item realistically. Aim to close one game and introduce another before interest has flagged.

Make sure the caterer is briefed on timing for eats and drinks. (Cold coffee can have a chilling effect on a programme!)

Check that all 'props' are assembled for games and skits well before the scheduled time of performance.

The leader can sometimes stretch a game if the kettle is not boiling, but in practice 'filling in' can often lose the interest of the group.

Do leave the hall or the house in as a clean a condition as you found it (or cleaner, if possible). Make sure that an adequate number of members have been briefed for this chore.

Alert certain people to look out for the retiring, shy person who may attend. If the event includes a number of strangers, plan to introduce them to someone at the start of the evening, who will make sure that they are introduced to others.

Plan a programme with the sex, age and relative ability of your guests in mind. The senior citizens may well be exhausted in a few minutes if too many active games are played!

Variety is the secret of a good party. Well-briefed leaders for each game or skit will ensure a good slick presentation and hold people's interest.

See further ideas for games in *Games Galore* (also published by Scripture Union) and in chapter 4

A competitive element—running the evening in teams or groups—can add extra excitement to the event. Choose names for each group, e.g. Crabs and Lobsters, Battleships and Bulldozers. If prizes must be awarded, make sure they are small and numerous—this can save embarrassment.

Prepare your committees for adaptability. The tempo and activities may need to be changed as the event progresses if 'deadness' is setting in.

3. Squashes

Usually this term implies a crowd squashed into a smallish room for some definite purpose, e.g. to hear a speaker, to see a demonstration or to launch a project. Wall games with suitable background music can be effectively used to break down initial reserve. Refreshments are usually taken standing up. 'Watch the carpet with that coffee!' The main event or speaker for the evening then follows. Speakers should be sympathetic to the often cramped conditions. Floors and chair arms can become hard if no limb movement is possible. Informality, friendship and involvement should be the keynotes.

4. Barbecues

Held in the open air, usually in the evening. A bonfire can be the centre around which participants congregate. Refreshments can be prepared over a single 'do-it-yourself' spit, using bricks to build a fireplace with metal strips forming a grill. A clean metal shoe scraper (from outside front door), odd oven racks or strong reinforcement mesh can be adapted to make a suitable area for barbecuing sausages, frying chips in pans or baking potatoes. Charcoal can usually be obtained from coal merchants or hardware stores. This material needs to be ignited in good time and requires a flow of air to keep the embers glowing.

The planning group should issue a note of invitation, stating what utensils participants should bring, e.g., fork, knife, plate, etc. Plastic cutlery can be obtained (dirty) in large quantities from motorway service areas, and washed.

The meal will be governed by the budget. We would suggest baked beans, burgers or sausages or, if you can afford luxuries, grilled steaks, chops or bacon. Remember the mustard, pickles and other condiments! Barbecues can be just socializing occasions or can be used for communicating some message. The aim will determine the overall programme. Games, fireworks, singing, a speaker, entertainment and group music can add much to a pleasurable evening. Have sufficient buckets of water on hand in case of emergency, and always make sure that the fire is extinguished after the event, especially if it has taken place on public property. It is wise to check with local authorities that fires are permitted on a public site.

5. Progressive meals

This is a youth group activity which demands the generosity of older friends, but often helps to bridge the generation gap. Prior arrangements are made for the group to have a glass of cordial or water at one house, soup at another, first course (not too elaborate) at the next, dessert and coffee at the two other venues. An excellent way of ensuring exercise is to have the venues a good distance apart. This can be worked out as a treasure or clue hunt. Another variation is 'map referencing'. Give participants a map reference for the road and number of the house. Divide into groups and, if possible, start them on the hunt from a variety of points.

6. Purposeful breakfasts

Valuable for unhurried consultations, Bible study or missionary groups. A simple breakfast is provided, followed by the projected activity. Appoint a chairman who has a reliable timepiece—some people do have to work. Make sure any speaker is well briefed as to the time available.

7. Coffee and dessert

For a large number who could never be entertained together for a whole meal, coffee and dessert may provide the starter for a friendship or fellowship evening. To save expense the 'price' of entry could be a bowl of dessert, handed in on arrival by a couple or small group.

8. Showers

Popular in the U.S.A. A group of friends who want to honour or celebrate a special occasion, invite a number of mutual friends (secretly). Each guest is invited to bring a suitable present to be given to the person to be honoured. A returning missionary, soldier, friend, newly-married pair, an

22

expectant mum or senior citizen who may be in need, arrive to find the group met together in his/her honour. Following refreshments, the surprised guest has presents 'showered' upon him/her. Be careful how you shower, especially if the honoured guest is frail!

9. One-sex dinners

'Father and Son', 'Mother and Daughter' occasions help to cement family relationships and provide platforms for communicating the Christian faith to one sex in a community.

The menu, table and hall decorations should be in the hands of a capable person. Dads and sons should be encouraged to sit together and to enjoy the friendship of similar pairs. An after-dinner speaker who does not speak 'down' to the sons or daughters, can provoke lively discussion between parents and children following the event.

10. Bible study groups

A renewed interest in the Bible has promoted many new groups. There is some excellent Bible study material available, particularly from Scripture Union and Inter-Varsity Press.

A small group of six to eight people often seems ideal. The leader should be thoroughly conversant with the selected passage, so that he can ask the group prepared positive questions. He must aim to stimulate, rather than dominate. To be firm, gracious and adaptable to the needs of the group.

Sitting around together, the leader should have the set passage read, perhaps twice, first from A.V. or R.S.V. and then from a modern paraphrase. He will have prepared by familiarizing himself with the historical background. After a short introduction, and a few minutes of quiet for the group to read over the passage a third time, ply the group with the first of a series of prepared questions, relating to the text. Avoid questions which can be answered by a straight 'yes' or 'no'. Application to contemporary life situations is important. Where there is an unsolved problem, set the group to finding out more information. Keep to the appointed length of time, allowing time to round off the study with a short summary by the leader or an elected member.

Much more could of course be said on this subject and is said very comprehensively in another Scripture Union paperback, *Your Turn To Lead*, by Margaret Parker. This is strongly recommended to all would-be group leaders.

11. This is Your Life

Research into the life of someone you wish to honour is very necessary in this project, but has its rich dividends. As with the T.V. programme, it is necessary to keep the evening a secret from the one whose life you are going to present, and by some devious way to bring the celebrity to the venue in time for the start of the programme.

Prior to this, records, photographs, letters, contacts with friends and relatives will have given you information to make up a book on the life of the honoured guest. The programme is enhanced if relatives and friends from some distance appear during the programme. The idea is to tell the story of a life, bringing in as many live instances as possible by getting friends to come on to the stage and to speak about their friend, reciting anecdotes about his or her life. Surprise is the essential ingredient. This activity is an excellent means of involving group members in research and performance. They need one major common gift—the gift of closed lips.

12. Exchange and mart

An evening given to the club or fellowship for exchanging hobbies, equipment, books, etc. This can be enormous fun, especially if the first part of the evening is given over to descriptions by each individual of the items which they wish to exchange or sell.

13. Valentine parties

February 14th gives a good excuse for a fun party with a particular slant. Games, programmes, refreshments can all bear the motif of hearts with arrows through them, and can prove an excellent social event.

14. Hallowe'en parties

Hallowe'en, the evening when witches supposedly fly on broomsticks. The myth needs to be exploded, but young people can enjoy the fantasy. Lanterns can be made out of vegetable swedes. This can be part of the evening's activity. The centre of the swede should be gorged out and apertures made for eyes, nose and mouth. Lighted candles can be placed inside these lanterns.

Games can have a witch flavour—relays on broomsticks, etc. Apple bobbing, where apples are placed in bowls of water and competitors have to try to bite at the apples with hands behind their backs. The best witches' hat competition, and the passing in the dark of objects in bags. After ten articles have been passed round the circle, lights go on and competitors write down the list of objects they felt. (See *Games Galore*, also published by Scripture Union, for other ideas.)

15. Talent spotting

Youth groups are always in need of talent for various jobs and social evenings. This can be discovered:
(a) by having a questionnaire with humorous, as well as serious, questions.
(b) by inviting all members to contribute to a special talent evening.
     Notice needs to be given so that adequate preparation can be made.

16. Eating contest

A variety of interesting contests can be held on one evening. Here are examples:
   Cream crackers and water, with a stipulation that for every glass of water two cream crackers must be eaten.
   Cold rice in bowls eaten off the floor, with participants kneeling and hands tied behind their backs.
   Raisins on plates to be eaten with tooth-picks.
   Peanuts eaten with knives and forks.
The variety is infinite. The more 'gooey' the substance, the greater the fun. But participants should be warned to come suitably dressed!

17. Exhibitions

Photography, art, handicrafts, cakes, confectionery and hobbies are intriguing, especially if enthusiasts speak for five minutes about their particular exhibit, e.g. the artist describes why a particular picture was painted, where, how long it took, etc.

18. Fancy Dress

An evening given to making fancy dresses can be quite creative. Each competitor is allowed to bring along a pre-scribed list of materials, e.g. ten newspapers, a gross of pins, a pint (or litre) of paint and the equipment for using these materials. A fashion parade should be held at the end of the evening with a carefully selected judging panel, and hilarious comment and laughter will inevitably ensue.

19. Cook-ins

Where there are gas or electric stoves, young people can be invited to bring specific ingredients to make a variety of dishes. Pastries, cakes and sweets could form the basis of gifts for older people in the district and there is plenty of fun and friendship generated for the participants.

20. Ping-pong competitions

These can either be of a 'knock-out' nature for single or doubles. With a large number it is best to limit it to one game per person in the early rounds.

Group ping-pong games can be quite hilarious. Six or eight participants are on each side of the table taking one hit of the ball and then passing the bat quickly to the next person, scoring in the usual way.

21. Holiday highlights

Films, filmstrips, pictures and narrated incidents bring much sunshine into a winter's evening. A member of the group can be invited to speak for two minutes on 'the most extra-ordinary experience of my holiday this year' or 'the oddest person I met this summer in Folkestone'.

22. Car rallies

Cryptic clues, often in rhymes and map references, are given on paper to each driver. Two or three panic envelopes with further instructions should be given in case of lost direction. Marks are forfeited for the number of envelopes opened. For further details, get in touch with your local car club; an enthusiast may volunteer to help you.

If there are a large number of participants, the routes can be varied, but all ending at a particular destination at a given time.

Refreshments and other activities can then take place at the venue.

23. Desert island discs

This popular radio series is useful for unravelling the story of someone's life. By careful prior consultation, the inter-viewee selects a number of records which have nostalgic or other associations in their lives. Two easy chairs and subdued lighting, good music reproduction, and an interviewer who is well briefed are essential. This is an excellent way of getting over a good story, or bringing out facts which perhaps a missionary or visiting notable person would be reticent to make known in public. Through questions and answers fairly deep probing is possible. You introduce the programme by giving the name of the person and stating that this is the choice which the victim is suggesting he or she would take with them on a desert island.

24. Caring and sharing

See chapter 7.

25. Community projects

Many councils are glad to have offers of voluntary service for running games, missions and adventure playgrounds. Application should be made to the local education authority. Hospitals, institutions, children's homes are often glad of group activities. Homes for the disabled and mentally retarded are glad of voluntary help, e.g. to take patients shopping, to share handicraft work and sports. (See chapter 7.)

26. Special speakers

Speakers can be obtained from many societies and associations on a very wide variety of subjects. For old or young people, such topics as Christianity and the Arts, Are Parents Really Necessary? or Children—an asset or liability? could be dealt with by convinced Christians. Your local M.P. may be willing to speak, as may a local Councillor or a Career Officer. Missionary Societies, some foreign Embassies, and many educational organizations are willing to supply speakers —and sometimes the local fire brigade, local C.I.D. and local branches of trade unions. It is advisable first to find out from organizations your commitment as to fees and expenses. Some may send speakers entirely free of charge; others—such as, for example, missionary societies—understandably expect the group to pay expenses.

27. Programme titles

A live group will require a duplicated or printed programme. This can be made more interesting if suitable titles can be found, and brain-storming sessions on programme titles can be a part of a social evening. Some extraordinary suggestions usually emerge.

28. Hobbies nights

Hobbies nights can be greatly enhanced if a specialist is invited to comment on the exhibits and perhaps to add his specialized knowledge on a particular subject. A great variety of clubs are often found in a given locality, and enthusiasts are only too willing to share their experiences.

29. Educational visits

Factories, commercial plants, banks, hospitals, homes for the elderly, sewage works and many other establishments arrange educational visits. These need to be planned well in advance. B.B.C. and Independent Television Studios are often open to small groups. Write, suggesting the programme you would like to view. 'If at first you don't succeed, try, try, try, again.'

30. Situational drama

In seeking to enthuse a group with a project, e.g. visiting old people, entertaining overseas students, a children's mission, etc., enthusiasm can often be raised by careful, short dramatic presentations of situations which may well arise within the project. For instance, if a visitation project is planned, three or four short demonstrations of the type of reaction which may be expected, over-emphasizing some of the negative aspects, can help people to see possibilities for the use of their own abilities. These can be extremely humorous and can be followed by group discussion, looking at the 'do's and don'ts' for the project.

31. The thing I dislike most, or pet aversions

Group members write on a paper their pet aversions or idiosyncrasies. The slips of paper are then put into a container and pulled out one by one. Members of the group guess whose pet aversion is being read out and, if the guess is right, the individual is called upon to explain his confession.

32. Crazy clue walks

Similar to a Treasure Hunt. The clues, however, have a crazy twist, e.g. At a public house 'The Oxtail' the clue could read—'Proceed till you see the soup of a kine which hangs behind, then turn right.'

33. Nature walks

The group have to locate a number of specified wild flowers, insects, birds, etc.—some to be collected, others to be observed and charted on a simple map. The winners are those who complete the course and return with the greatest number of required objects. Preparation is essential. Be careful not to ask them to locate a woodpecker which you may have seen on one of your walks around a particular route—they have a habit of flying away! It may be best to devise a points system, so that, for example, you get more points for spotting a woodpecker than you do for picking a dandelion.

34. Scavenger hunts

An excellent quick exercise for clearing a field after games is to offer a small prize for the boy or girl who can find, say, fifty whole sweet wrappers. A more sophisticated hunt can take in a much wider area. Participants are given a list of the booty which they must collect. A variation on this is to give crazy clues.

35. Work and faith

Many interesting speakers are usually available in an area, and Christians can be asked to speak on the theme of Work and Faith. Often this opens up new vistas of understanding as to possible jobs for young people, and the reality of the person's living faith can bring great strength, courage and hope to a teenager. This item can help to promote understanding amongst members of the community.

A variation on this is for actual members fof the group to speak about their jobs. This promotes friendship and leads to a deeper community spirit being created within the group. It often leads on to discussion concerning opportunities, problems and inadequacies which people have felt.

36. My last chance

A word picture is created. Four members of the group or audience are invited to share a raft in mid-Atlantic. As their plight becomes more desperate, it is quite obvious that the raft can only support one person adequately and supplies of food must run out. Each of the four makes a speech in which he seeks to persuade the others that he has the greatest contribution to make to society, and that he should therefore be the one to stay on the raft and not voluntarily go overboard. This programme can have a semi-serious slant, e.g. if you suggest four professions, e.g. a doctor, a minister of religion, a great conductor or musician, a millionaire philanthropist—or a humorous twist, e.g. Father Christmas, Snow White, Donald Duck, Yogi Bear.

37. Electioneering

Four or five of the group members have put up for Parliament. They prepare speeches (give a week's warning) on subjects of interest to the community. On the group evening, each candidate is allotted a certain time to speak. He can be heckled and questioned by the audience. At the end of the evening, the election is held when the members judge the best candidate. This should be very light-hearted and the subjects for the speeches should have a humorous twist, e.g.

Policemen should have larger boots.
Television should be banned for a year.
Women should be heard and not seen.

38. Every voice debate

Two teams are arranged facing each other, a Chairman sitting at the end of the two rows. Team leaders of (*a*) and (*b*) announce the motion which the house is going to debate, and going down each row, each person has to give one reason why he supports the motion, while the other side gives reasons for opposing the motion. The debate continues with each alternate side having a voice, e.g.

(*a*)1. Will speak for the motion.
(*b*)1. Will speak against.
(*a*)2. Will give his reason
(*b*)2. Will oppose

To add to the fun, each member must stand before he speaks. By this means all members of the group have to get to their feet and say something, which is often a great help to the more retiring members. Humorous topics should be included, e.g. 'All beards should be banned.'

39. Hereby hangs a tail

Selected members are briefed to prepare short papers on given subjects. Preferably something which has interested them, a hobby or a pet aversion, and in the course of their presentation they demonstrate how their hobby or their pet aversion has led them into some embarrassing or some extraordinary situation. This can either be a true story or something fictional. The stories are judged at the end of the evening, and the applause by the audience indicates the winner.

Variation
Give the participants a phrase which either they must explain in their story, suggesting its origin, or which they must weave in to their talk in some devious way.

40. Find the team member

This activity is excellent for camps and children's missions, especially in seaside or country areas. Well-known team members dress in disguise and take up positions in a given area, e.g. as a window cleaner busy up a ladder, an old gentleman sitting in the park allegedly asleep with a paper over his face, an engineer underneath a car, a nurse pushing a pram, a holiday maker dozing in the sun with large dark glasses, or even a parson on visits in the locality. There is no end of the possibilities. The competitors have a paper which has to be signed when they discover one of the team members. They only receive the signature, however, if they ask a question which has previously been agreed by the team, e.g. 'Are you a white elephant?' 'Are you a black beetle?' If the question is correctly phrased, then the disguised worker must sign the paper. A time limit is fixed, and the person with the largest number of signatures at the end of the game is the winner.

41. Overseas visitors

Entertaining overseas visitors at a Youth Club or fellowship can be extremely good fun and very informative. If a small group from one country can be contacted and invited to share an evening, they will very often make good suggestions for one of their national meals, and some may even come in national dress. After-dinner talks by the visitors can be most illuminating and humorous. This is not only good for the club, but it is excellent for establishing relationships with students and other overseas visitors who often feel quite lonely and cut off from the reserved English. Films from

Embassies and Tourist boards are often very good background material, and can usually be secured for the price of postage.

42. Films

Many excellent films are available from a host of distributors on a wide variety of themes. Many commercial organizations, embassies and tourist boards have free film services. Careful preparation and installation of equipment is essential if the performance is to have a semi-professional air. Pre-recorded music, playing as the audience assembles, and limited lighting which can be dimmed at the commencement of the show, add to the sense of occasion. (See Appendix for distributors and sources of films.)

43. Story scopes

Leader holds up a 'scope machine' made out of a box with mirrors and knobs. This completely useless object can have twinkling torch lights which flash on when operated. Leader looks into 'Box' and begins to relate a story (Bible, fairy or other well-known story). Participants have to guess the event or title as the leader unfolds the details. Can be played in groups on a competition basis, or rewards can be given to the first individual to give the correct answer.

44. Humorous dog shows

A humorous dog show can be hilarious. Organize a suitable showing ring, appoint judges who are canine addicts, print a programme listing the classes.
  These could include:
  The dog with the waggiest tail—the most obedient dog—the most disobedient dog—the dog with the best smile—the loudest bark—pronounced waddle—ugliest face—cutest ears—longest tongue, etc.
  The event should be well organized, competitors bearing numbers. The M.C. must be certain of the order of entries

33

and must announce carefully the number of the competitor and name of the dog competing, as they enter the ring. A good public-address system is essential—a crowd of dogs really is worse than a clutch of hens for noise. Sufficient marshals should be appointed and their duties carefully defined, e.g. stewarding, spectators, marshalling competitors, catching strays (!) and keeping records at the judges' table.

Prizes can be given, together with rosettes.

45. House parties

Many young teenagers often make many discoveries on well-organized week-end group house-parties or longer group holidays. Eating and sleeping under the same roof are great levellers. You can't live at close quarters with your friends without self-discovery and also often embarrassment or challenge. Community living—peeling the 'spuds' together, playing together, worshipping together, snoring together in the dorm, and washing in the communal bath-house can really sandpaper off some of the awkward corners of our personalities.

Party-holidays can be relatively inexpensive. Early booking of a centre is usually essential. It is advisable to plan at least twelve months ahead. Plan the programme carefully and encourage full participation. Party rates are available on many items and, if you are catering, 'bulk rates' can be a significant saving. Unobtrusive discipline will make for a good atmosphere. Rules, though few, may need to be spelt out and reasons given. This will contain or curb undue pranks which can, if prolonged, be a nuisance and embarrassment. A tactful word at the beginning of the project about the property or the canvas may save expensive bills for damages. Smaller clubs can often join with larger groups to mutual advantage.

There are some excellent centres available on the continent. With careful organizing it is often possible to meet people of a comparable age and with similar interests in a number of overseas centres.

Adequate insurance should be negotiated for personal and party equipment.

46. Talks on health education and sex

Because of all the pressures on young people today, an evening or a series of gatherings on these subjects can be extremely useful. The gospel of Jesus is concerned about wholeness. A healthy appreciation of the role of sex in human life can be very emancipating. Single chastity and married fidelity are Christian values which need careful explanation. A Christian Welfare Officer or local doctor will often be prepared to co-operate. The Central Council for Health Education will supply films and filmstrips.

47. Come-back night

A chance to invite all past members for a reunion—it can be nostalgic and also rewarding. Make sure the programme is worthy of the present membership! Ensure name tags are provided. A chance for an 'I remember . . .' session by the 'oldies' can be included, often with entertaining results.

48. Careers and callings

Invite individuals from varied backgrounds who hold interesting jobs to talk about their life at work. Socially these can be creative sessions and can give helpful information and incentive to the young people at a formative time of their lives.

Here are a few suggestions:

A Press Photographer
A Monkey Keeper or Lion Keeper from the Zoo
Entertainer or Clown
A Surgeon or other member of the Medical Profession
A Welfare Officer
A Magistrate
A Missionary
A Creative Artist
A Town Clerk
A Farmer
A Housewife
A Broadcaster
An Author

The list can be endless, but try to find information about interesting speakers by questioning people you know.

Brief each speaker clearly, giving details about your group (including age range, some indications as to educational level and interests, etc.), set out the time-table for the meeting, ask the speaker whether he or she is prepared to answer questions at the end of the talk, and discover whether he or she would like to use any equipment, e.g. a slide projector.

The leader or chairman of the meeting should be given a one-paragraph or so biography of the speaker, so that he or she can be introduced accurately and interestingly. It is also appropriate to end the meeting with a vote of thanks from a member of the audience and this should be planned in advance.

49. 'Six Feet Above Criticism' or 'Gas and Gaiters'

An opportunity to quiz a local parson or minister on his work, ministry—or his sermons. It is amazing how human and un-parsonic the preacher becomes by the end of the session!

50. Sound and Slide

There is so much photographic material around that is just waiting to be used creatively. It is an effective means of communication and entertainment. Give groups the task of presenting their own themes. Slides can be set to pre-recorded music and commentary. Songs can be illustrated by a series of slides. Two projectors can be focused on one screen so that no break occurs in projection. Epilogues with Scripture readings, music and visual slides can be extremely effective, but selection and careful presentation are essential. Many have suffered poor quality slides and commentary by an enthusiastic holiday picture taker. Try your hand at being more creative by careful selections and preparation. Professional slides can be obtained from Woodmansterne Ltd., Holywell Industrial Estate, Watford, WD1 82D. (Send for a brochure.)

Chapter 4

Entertainments
Skits and Mini-Pantomimes
for Socials, Camps and Parties

Introduction

It is the claim of Christianity that the spirit of Jesus Christ liberates the whole man, bringing freedom and a positive joy. Yet one of the strange hang-ups which has often bugged Christians has been their attitude to drama, the theatre and entertainment in general. However, since the advent of television, which has brought its art forms into our drawing rooms, many Christians have had to re-think their position.

For some, television has been the pathway to hypocrisy. They have deep reservations about attending live shows, but are avid viewers of most programmes on the small screen. This discrepancy has been noted, and has received outspoken comment from many of the younger generation. The theatre has been a vexed subject—'to go or not to go?'—that is the question. This has often been tantamount to a test of orthodoxy or spirituality. A case can be argued for saying that the theatre has not always been the most moral of institutions in Britain, but this is a generalization. Discussion and controversy as to a Christian attitude to the arts, and in particular as to what constitutes art or pornography, is seemingly endless, though in the whole area of the arts, Prof. Rookmaaker's work and some of the insights of Dr. Francis Schaeffer have been extremely helpful in recent years.

In establishing guidelines it is becoming increasingly clear that a number of Christians have a general intolerance of, and often an irrational prejudice against drama. The church is therefore bereft of talent to convey God's truth in this audio-visual age.

But to speak of drama as in itself an unworthy medium is surely misguided. And in a day when so much of our learning takes place through visual media, those who want to communicate any message will need to reflect again on the place of the dramatic. And of course the Bible itself is full of drama. The Tabernacle in the Old Testament was a visual aid to the Children of Israel—and an expensive one! The pillar of smoke, the cloud by day and the fire by night, displayed the presence of an almighty God. The prophets often acted their message, and when Jesus came on the scene, He so often taught people by asking them to lift up their eyes and look around them. The Gospel is drama, poetry and prose, and all these and music have a part to play in our cultural development, and we need to consider using all these in our celebration of God's gifts in worship.

One of the contradictions in some Christians is that they are willing to share in rumbustious skits and stunts for entertainment purposes, and yet they shun more serious drama. But so often the serious professional playwright prompts and stimulates thinking. Should we not consider more serious drama as an opportunity for opening a discussion? Why not visit the theatre in small groups to view a carefully selected play and then another evening get together to discuss its essential message, its challenge, its value? Drama can be evocative and can lead to self-discovery. Obviously the play to be seen must be chosen carefully, both for its quality and for the depth and relevance of the issues that it raises.

The entertainment skits which are included in this book depend on spontaneity and total involvement. For most of them exaggerated actions are essential, and costumes should be extravagant and ridiculous.

When you read these brief scripts your first reaction may well be 'What corny stuff!' But bear in mind that comedy skits rely on their actions, not on their words, and that these scripts are but the skeletons which can be clothed with much ad libbing and as many local references as possible. Even the Goon Show scripts made corny reading as compared with the actual radio broadcasts in which they were performed.

So we suggest that you read over these basic comedies and adapt and improve them for use in your local situation.

1. We Want Fireworks

Purpose—to rouse audience participation. Suitable for all ages, but particularly for children.

You will need a series of cards prepared with the following titles, large enough for the audience to read easily.

1. AH
2. WHISTLE
3. HOORAY
4. SHSHSHSH
5. CLAP
6. SSSSS
7. WE WANT FIREWORKS

You will also need some people (hidden) with balloons and pins. The leader has the cards in his hand and shows them one by one. Whatever is on the card the audience must do or say. He can make this as brief or as long as he desires. Have a trial run and on the second performance, the surprise ending, quite unexpected by the audience, occurs when they have cried out 'We want fireworks' and certain confederates behind a curtain or screen have burst balloons with pins (or, in the open air, have let off fireworks). The loud report ensures a good laugh.

2. Wreck of the *Hesperus*

Suitable for children and young people. Aim—group participation and breaking down reserve.

You will need flip cards with the words in capitals which are used to get audience participation. A story-teller should display them at the appropriate time. Instruct the audience about volume; the story-teller's fist being waved frantically means that they shout the words loudly; his open hand patting downwards indicates a whispered response. The performance is easier if an assistant exhibits the cards at the appropriate time. The following story can be expanded at will:

The good ship *Hesperus* was slowly ploughing through a smooth sea reflecting blue from the cloudless sky, her white sails billowing gently before a steady breeze (**AD LIB**). Suddenly the breeze stiffened and a small cloud appeared over the horizon. The sea became choppy and the ship rocked from side to side. Higher the wind rose, and large foreboding clouds appeared. The tall masts were plunging to and fro, half hidden beneath the mounting waves. Then the thunder roared and soon a full-scale storm raged round the ship. The wind blew strong

Hold up first flash card

(*1st half children*)   WWHHEE . . . WWHHEE . . .

and the waves thundered down.

(*2nd flash card*)

(*2nd half children*)   SPLASH . . . SPLASH . . .

Soon the ship ground to a sudden shuddering halt.

(*3rd flash card*)   CRASH . . . CRASH

It had struck a rock. Soon the voices rang out

Flash Card (*1st half children*)   Shiver me timbers, the ship is sinking

Flash Card (*2nd half children*)   Shiver me timbers, we'll all get drowned

The Captain shouted the order

   Lower the lifeboats, lower the lifeboats

and the bosun's whistle sounded

Flash Card   EEEP . . . EEP

Soon the men were at their places by the lifeboats and the bosun shouted

(*1st half children*)   Down a bit, down a bit,

(*2nd half children*)   Not too 'ard, not too 'ard.

(*1st half children*)   Crash

(*2nd half children*)   Too 'ard (quietly disappointed)

The lifeboats landed in the water and the cry went up

   Women and children first, women and children first.

Soon the lifeboats were filled and you could hear the crew straining at the oars

(*1st half children*)   EE PLIP . . . EEE PLIP . . . EEE PLIP

(*Small group*)

Perhaps you wonder what the plip was. There was a little bit of leather loose at the end of one of the rowlocks so that after the oar moved it plipped into place. They gradually rowed away over the horizon to the shore.

(*1st half children*) gradual diminuendo EEE PLIP EEE PLIP EEE PLIP

(*Small group*)

Soon the storm died down and there was nothing to be seen but the smooth sea reflecting the blue cloudless sky.

3. The scratching tramp

You will need a park bench which can be made of a plank on two chairs. A vagrant, suitably dressed, is stretched out on the length of the bench, sleeping. A city gent comes in, pokes him and tells him to move up as he wants to sit down. The vagrant bends his knees and shuffles a short way down the seat, giving just enough room for the gent to sit down.

A sporty gent then enters, digs the beggar in the ribs, and tells him to 'Move along, old boy.' Vagrant doubles up and the sporty gent takes his seat on the bench.

These are followed in turn by a well-upholstered lady and another gent who go through the same procedures to get a seat.

Eventually the vagrant has but a few inches on the end of the bench. When everyone is smiling and is seemingly content, the vagrant starts to scratch himself. The character nearest to him starts to scratch and gets up in disgust and moves off. The vagrant takes up more of the bench. Again he begins to scratch and to search for fleas. The lady, seeing this, begins to feel uncomfortable, and she begins to itch and scratch and eventually, in disgust, she gets up and moves off.

Each character in turn follows suit and the skit ends with the vagrant smiling and going off to sleep occupying the whole length of the bench.

4. No rest for the wicked

You will need a park bench, as in 3 above.

A man is lying on a bench, snoozing and enjoying a quiet sleep in the sun. Enter a lively character talking about the beautiful day, the roseate hues and the prolific purple poppies. Then he says in a clear voice 'Could you please tell me the time?' The man on the bench says he hasn't a watch and bids him good-day.

A second intruder comes in, says 'good afternoon' and asks for the time. The man on the bench answers that he has no watch and doesn't know the time.

The second intruder is followed in turn by any number of characters asking the same question. The man on the bench obviously becomes annoyed, and across his newspaper and with a felt pen he writes 'I don't know the time.' He holds this up so that the audience can see what he has written.

He then lies out full length on the bench with the paper over his face. A dog-collared parson comes on to the scene, looks at the man, and reads aloud what he has written over his newspaper: 'I don't know the time.' Then digs him in the ribs, wakes him up while looking at his watch, and says 'My dear man, it is five o'clock' and then walks off. The man on the bench gets up in a rage and, tearing paper in shreds, leaves the platform.

5. Fred's dead

You will need the following characters:
1. Fred, the husband
2. Aggie, his wife, preferably with curlers in her hair
3. The doctor with a bag, stethoscope and top hat
4. The undertaker with a black bowler hat or other suitable insignia
5. The parson attired in dog collar and glasses on end of nose
6. The film producer

The compere sets the scene:

He tells the audience—'This is a film set, and the cast is practising to make a very solemn yet popular film.'

The producer shouts: 'Shoot 1—Scene 1.'

Fred collapses on the stage. His wife rushes to him, turns him over, looks at his face, feels his pulse, and says in a slow manner 'Fred's dead! Call the doctor, call the doctor!'

The doctor comes in with slow step, examines the patient and announces in solemn tones, 'Fred is dead. Call the undertaker!'

The undertaker solemnly approaches the scene, head bowed. Walks three times round the body, shaking his head, and saying 'Fred's dead, Fred's dead. We'd better call the parson.'

The parson comes in, acknowledges the bow of Mrs., the doctor and the undertaker, takes a long look at Fred, and slowly in a high pitched voice says 'Poor Fred is dead.'

Producer shouts 'Cut. That was much too slow. The audience will go to sleep. Let's go through the scene much more quickly!'

The scene is then re-enacted at at least twice the pace, everyone doing things at the double. At the end, producer again cries 'Cut' and says 'That was better. A little too fast, but we shall have them all crying. Let's put some humour into it.'

The whole scene is repeated at a medium pace, but everyone, when they say 'Fred is dead' has a great laugh. The scene ends with producer crying 'Cut, cut, cut', and laughing.

This skit can have as many variations as desired.

6. The ugliest man in the world

(Man standing at back of stage, engulfed in a blanket, with his back to the audience.)

Compere: We have here the ugliest man in the world. I dare anyone in the audience to come up and see him (or should I say it) face to face.

(First pre-elected volunteer—someone well known to audience, if possible—goes up, sees ugliest man, screams and drops 'dead' on to the stage.)

Compere: Oh dear! You've seen what's happened. We dare anyone in the audience to come up and look at him.

(Second pre-elected volunteer repeats above and drops 'dead.')

Compere: To look at this man and stay alive, one must be a man of fortitude, so could Mr . . . come up.

(He comes up, looks at the ugliest man. Ugliest man drops 'dead.')

7. Court laughs

First entry, with suitcase
Leader: Hello, Mr. X. What are you doing with that suitcase?
Mr. X: What am I doing with my suitcase?
Leader: Yes, what are you doing with that suitcase?
Mr. X: Oh, I'm taking my case to court.
Second entry, with ladder
Leader: Hello Mr. X. What are you doing with that ladder? etc.
Mr. X: I'm taking my case to a higher court.
Third entry, with bell

Leader: Hello Mr. X. What are you doing with that bell? etc.
Mr. X: I'm taking my case to the court of appeal.

8. First date

You will need three people: one to tell the story while the other two act it. Story-teller describes getting up in the morning, washing, cleaning teeth, eating cornflakes, etc. (make up own dialogue)

Two Actors: One sits on chair with other on his lap, with a coat covering them. First person's arms are through arms of coat. First person (underneath) is doing action without being able to see what he is doing, this gives impression of a dwarf. The face of No. 2 is being washed and fed, etc., by the arms and hands of No. 1, who, of course, cannot see. The whole thing is amusing and can be messy!

9. Mixed up broadcasting

You will need quick and reasonably good readers. Mock up a broadcasting studio. Microphones and a red light give an air of authenticity. Mugs can be used to speak into to obtain the broadcast effect, but the voices must at all times be audible. Though pauses must be allowed for laughter, each speaker must follow the others quickly. Mixed lines can be extremely entertaining, but there is need for careful rehearsal before the event.

Compere: One night the radio was not functioning very well, for it picked up four talks at the same time. These talks were given by a doctor, a bus driver, a cookery expert and a musician. They speak in that order.

A Good evening, everybody, I must say

B Good evening, listeners, allow me to say

C Good evening, listeners, before I begin my talk tonight, may I say

D Good evening, listeners. Let us continue our talk on music

A Which is enough to give any child a bad cold. To relieve a cold on the lungs, rub the child's chest with

B Ethyl which has passed the government analysis; but we bus drivers run on a commercial grade, which, of course,

44

is much cheaper. A liberal amount of oil should be used when

C   Making shortbread, as this gives crispness when cooked. To make Irish stew take 1 lb. of steak, 2 lbs. of potatoes

B   And one tin of carbide mixed with water. This gives off a highly inflammable gas which is

A   Excellent for bronchitis, pneumonia and housemaid's knee

D   and other musical instruments. You will notice the rest in the first bar. While waiting you should

B   Fill your radiator with

C   Rice pudding until it is

A   Unconscious. Lie the child on its back

B   Make sure the petrol and air are shut off

C   And add sugar and milk to taste

D   And run up and down the scales

C   Using them to weigh the raisins or currants

B   Of electricity which light the car. If this fails to work

C   Stir for half an hour and

A   Gargle the nose and mouth

B   And other prominent parts with Harpol or Brasso, which add the finishing touch. Should the brakes refuse to act, change down to bottom gear, engage the clutch, and

D   Whistle 'Home Sweet Home' until

A   The doctor arrives. Hot fomentations placed on the

B   Self-starter greatly assist starting. It is wise

C   To take a spoonful of bisurated magnesia mixed with

B   A gallon of petrol

C   Cover down and place in a hot oven and you will

D   Quickly learn to play the harp. The best way to reach the top notes is

A   To have an operation for the adenoids and tonsils, and carefully

B   Scrape your gears. This is often done when learning to drive. If, while you are driving, the engine ceases to fire, this may be due to lack of petrol or an oily plug or

A   An unwise consumption of

C   Stale dough

D   Me, soh, doh in tonic sol far. Before beginning to sing, take care to

B   Drain the crank case

A And take a large dose of castor oil

C About every half hour as an average

D This will remove all doubts from the mind. Keep your voice in a

A Bottle tightly corked, and shake well before using.

D Which gives a beautiful tremulo effect. My time is

B Kept under the cushion in the back seat of the car. Be sure always to carry an adjustable spanner, preferably a large one, in case

A the patient becomes troublesome. A tap now and then is all that is

C Kneaded to keep it light and spongy. Pots and pans should be kept

B Spotlessly clean with an oily rag. A grease gun will be found useful

C For icing Christmas and Birthday cakes. Fill carefully with pink icing sugar

A And place in the patient's ear, then syringe well. If you do not possess a syringe of your own, you may

B Borrow a foot pump from any garage. Having done this, take the handle firmly, press towards the ear until it engages and the engine

A Will cough, vomit or splutter, in which case the

D piano will need tuning. Good

A Night

C Every

B Body

10. Mixed up lines 2

You will need three quick and reasonably good readers, and the same props as for Item 9 above. This time, the three speakers are:

    A Desert Island Discs Compere

    A Cookery Expert

    A Hobbies Expert

Cookery Expert: How to bake a perfect cake

Hobbies Expert: And make a model aircraft

Desert Island Discs Compere: What does your choir enjoy doing?

C.E.: Breaking eggs and dropping them into the flour. Mix well and

H.E.: Stick it firmly together with glue. You next take the

D.I.D.: Children up to the top notes. We found that we enjoyed singing when we became

C.E.: A pinch of salt. Then, when this is absorbed, add

H.E.: A small pin through the nose of the plane. This will hold the

D.I.D.: Audience in their seats. We made a record and sold it to

C.E.: Some dried fruit. An extra taste is obtained

H.E.: By painting the model grey and the title of an Airline Company on

D.I.D.: Their parents. I understand that you have participated in

C.E.: Stirring it up until it reaches a smooth consistency. Then take the baking tin

H.E.: And cut a half inch slip in the base for the

D.I.D.: Next piece of music I would like to hear is

C.E. Greaseproof paper. Pour the mixture in carefully, making sure that it reaches

H.E.: The undercarriage of the aircraft. Fit the tailpiece in the

D.I.D.: Back of my mind and it brings back such pleasant

C.E.: Edges and is flat on top. Put the oven on very hot and

H.E.: Watch it sail up in the air. You have now made

D.I.D.: A big thank-you for coming to the studio tonight and all of us in the studio wish you and your choir

C.E.: A perfect cake and

H.E.: A lovely aeroplane of which you can truly be proud.

11. I want to be an actor

You will need a short humorous play, twelve actors and a compere. The aim of this activity is amusement, coupled with talent spotting. The compere introduces the item, stating that a new play has been written for radio, and that three reader-actors are required for the main parts. Auditions to take place immediately. Twelve people are auditioned for the three parts.

Actors are chosen on merit, and this is indicated by the length and volume of the applause from the audience. For each main character three people are auditioned. They come to the microphone and read two or three lines from the script and the applause is measured.

Having elected the three actors from the twelve possibles, the audience is then invited to choose the best actor, who is to receive an Oscar at the end of the evening. The play is then read and the best actor chosen by the above means. Select the compere carefully, as he is the secret of success.

12. One actor—three parts

You will need three hats which indicate to the audience the character being acted.

Introduction to audience

At great expense we had engaged a troupe of players to be with us this evening to produce the fabulous story of Sir Lancelot. Unfortunately they missed their bus at Waterloo (or some such locally famed transport departure point) and so with great courage, fortitude and an overplus of enthusiasm we have prevailed upon Mr . . . to act the three parts of our drama.

May I introduce yo you:

(*The actor, taking hat No. 1, is then introduced as 'Sir Lancelot.' Sir Gasper, Sir Lancelot's deadly rival, is introduced by the actor placing another hat on his head.*

The maiden in distress is finally introduced, preferably with a large garden-party-type lady's hat.

As the story-teller relates the tale, so the one actor mimes with great gusto the various parts, changing hats at the appropriate time.

The story-teller needs to watch the antics of the actor carefully and to pause when there is audience laughter.

Numerous variations with local references can be incorporated, or local stories can be written and adapted.)

One day as Sir Lancelot was riding his trusty steed, Archibald, along the South Deeside Road, he saw his deadly rival Sir Gasper running off along the Gimoc by-pass with a fair maiden prostrate under his arm.

The blonde was obviously in great distress and was quothing 'Help! Help!' as Sir Gasper pounded along.

'Marry' quoth Sir Lancelot, for that was what Sir Gasper

obviously intended to do, and spurred his steed to greater efforts. Sir Gasper, looking over his shoulder, saw Sir Lancelot closing on him fast. He raced for his castle gates. But Sir Lancelot soon got within average-size battle-axe range, and taking his average-size battle-axe from his pocket, he whirled it three times around his head and threw it after Sir Gasper. But Sir Gasper happened to turn his head and saw it coming. He ducked quickly so that it whistled over his left ear. 'Phew,' quoth he, and 'phew again. That was a close shave.' Which indeed it was, for it removed half his beard. Meanwhile the blonde, with her bird's eye view of Sir Gasper's horse's galloping feet, trembled as the axe whistled overhead. Still Sir Lancelot urged on his trusty one-horse-power steed, which he was still buying on the HP, and slowly gained on Sir Gasper. He raised his trusty lance and threw, but again Sir Gasper, glancing round, saw it coming and swerved into his castle gates, as the lance buried itself in the portcullis. 'Phew,' said Sir Gasper, 'that was a very close shave,' which it was, for it removed the other half of his beard.

Up the tower of the castle raced Sir Gasper, pulling the unfortunate blonde behind him. Up the castle steps raced the unfortunate blonde in the grip of the dastardly Sir Gasper, who was meanwhile racing up the steps clutching the unfortunate maiden, who was meanwhile racing up the steps, being pulled by the dastardly Sir Gasper, who was etcetera.

'Marry,' quoth Sir Lancelot again, as he raced up the steps after Sir Gasper, for that unhappy event was obviously drawing near.

Up the stairs of the tower raced Sir Gasper, pulling behind him the blonde, who was sobbing her heart out. Sir Lancelot, racing behind, picked it up, so he could return it at the earliest opportunity.

Sir Gasper burst into the turret room. He pulled himself together (again) and, throwing the unfortunate maiden against the far wall, where she landed with a loud 'splat,' he hurled himself against the door. Sir Lancelot, racing up the stairs behind, just got his foot in the door in time. Sir Gasper shoved with all his might, his left shoulder appearing at his right-hand side with the strain, but Sir Lancelot got his foot and his knee and his shoulder into the gap. Sir Gasper pushed, Sir Lancelot got his head into the gap, Sir Gasper heaved.

Sir Lancelot replaced his head and burst into the room, scattering caution to the winds. He drew his trusty broad sword and aimed an almighty blow at Sir Gasper's head. Sir Gasper ducked and, drawing his battle axe, swiped at Sir Lancelot. Sir Lancelot side-stepped and thrust at Sir Gasper's heart; but he, with an almighty blow, snapped his sword in two. Sir Lancelot threw the useless end into the corner, where the sobbing maiden just ducked in time. What would Sir Lancelot do now? Sir Gasper prepared for the final blow. Sir Gasper aimed the final blow (Actor: GET ON WITH IT). Suddenly Sir Lancelot had a brainwave, he drew his trusty fist and hurled it at Sir Gasper's chin, following clumsily in its wake as he did so. He, that is Sir Gasper, managed a short 'Goodness gracious me!' as he collapsed on the floor. Sir Lancelot picked him up and threw him through the window. He fell head over heels over the rampart and plunged towards the moat below.

The blonde swooned to the floor, quothing endearing quoths. 'Come, my love,' quoth Sir Lancelot and, picking her up, they walked arm in arm down the stairs. They arrived at the bottom just in time to see Sir Gasper landing in the moat, his parachute billowing above him.

13. One actor, three parts—variation

Narrator explains that a team of actors from Outer Mongolia have just arrived in this country at much cost to the organizers, but somehow they have lost their twenty-nine wagons of scenery and props, which are now circling somewhere in the middle of the Siberian desert. Nevertheless, at tremendous expense, the organizers have persuaded someone to deputise for the whole troupe.
Narrator continues:
I gladly introduce to you our one actor who will take all three parts. Each different actor is distinguished by a particular hat. First, Father John, who is over-concerned about the safety of his daughter. Actor places a bowler hat on his head.

Secondly, the daughter's lover. Actor swops his bowler for a cap.

Thirdly, Father John's beautiful, delectable, desirable yet

diffident daughter, Anthea. The actor puts on a flowery floppy hat and bows to the audience.

Our story begins with Father John sitting in his palatial stately home in Stowe-on-the-Mud. Crickets creak outside the window. The wind blows through the darkened night. The doors creak on their hinges. The cows moan as their noses sense that snow is in the air. (Appropriate sounds—over emphasized—can be made.) Father John and daughter Anthea eat their frugal meal of sardines-twice-removed-on-toast. But hark, there is another sound breaking through the air—the stealthy footsteps of Anthea's lover, who is now creeping up to the stately home where Father John and daughter Anthea sit at their ten-foot table, eating their sardines. The cat purrs in the corner, the dog barks, the hyena howls. The lover continues to approach stealthily through the long, long grass. The owl hoots, breaking the slience of the night. Father John starts—Anthea swallows a sardine whole. Anthea's lover creeps towards the window. Anthea says to Father John, 'Let me take your empty plate now to the kitchen.' Her lover, watching through a chink in the curtains, moves quickly round the building. Anthea carries her father's plate through the massive oak door, and runs down the fifty-foot hall to the kitchen. Anthea's lover outside the building sees what she is doing and runs down to the kitchen window. Anthea comes through the kitchen door. The lover shields his eyes as the light is turned on. He sees his opportunity. Anthea goes to the washing-up machine and places her father's plate, turning on the tap and pressing the electric button. Stealthily, her lover creeps through the massive kitchen door. Anthea, concentrating on the washing-up, doesn't comprehend the danger of the situation. Suddenly the lover grasps her round the waist. She turns, furious, and faints. He picks her up, and takes her through the dark night down through the creaking trees.

Anthea wakes from her faint, and screams. The lover now runs with his heavy burden slung across his shoulders in a fireman's lift. He reaches the end of the drive, but Father John has heard the noise. He's up—he grasps his gun, and running down the drive, sees Anthea on the lover's two-seater bicycle, pedalling away in the direction of the M.1. Father John rushes round to the garage, jumps into his battered

Bentley and gives chase. The lover pedals furiously. Anthea faces him tentatively. Father John drives speedily, his old bones rattling as the Bentley bumps its way over the pot-holes of Poodle Lane. The lover has now stopped. He is on the bridge over the M.1. He sees Father John rapidly approaching. The lover is determined that this time daughter Anthea shall be his. Father John is equally determined that his priceless, pretty, provocative daughter shall not leave the family homestead. The Bentley pulls up to a halt. The lover shouts 'Stop! Not a pace nearer.' Father John walks on. The lover picks up daughter Anthea and dangles her over the bridge, threatening to drop her on to the traffic. Father John is frightened—stops dead in his tracks. Streaming up the M.1 comes the noble British Army, the convoy moving slowly. The lover thinks that the Army is after him and suddenly takes fright and drops Anthea. Down she goes and lands in a grateful sergeant's arms. The lorries come on. One after another they pass under the bridge. The lover is so annoyed that he jumps and lands on the turret of a tank. Father John looks over the bridge and at his daughter being carried away still in the arms of the sergeant. He faints, flops, and toppling over the bridge he lands with splattering and spluttering on to the lap of the ensuing General.

The Actor collapses on stage breathless. Gradually he recovers, puts on the three hats and takes his bow.

14. Peanut butter

Scene. A group of four or five workmen are on stage—whistle is blown for lunch break.

Act 1. Each takes out his lunch bag—the contents can be varied, strings of sausages, lots of imitation eggs and cakes for a 'fat' person, an austerity lunch for a 'thin' character. The principal character is last to unwrap carefully, with great determination, a small packet of sandwiches. Looking into the open packet he scowls and groans, 'PEANUT Butter,' and hurls the sandwiches to the ground. Others look on with some concern.

Act 2. Same procedure as Act 1—Main character smiles as he carefully opens his sandwiches, scowls and shouts 'PEA-

52

NUT Butter'—hurls the sandwich away, in disgust—others look astonished and shake their heads.

Act 3. Same as Acts 1 and 2, but closing with a workman butting in saying 'Hey mate, excuse my saying so, why don't you tell your wife you don't like peanut butter?'

Main character (angrily): You leave my wife out of this. I make my own sandwiches.

Curtain.

15. Mini-miming pantomimes

These are good fun items. Played by a camp staff or a group of organization leaders, they can prove very good entertainment with a minimum of preparation.

Miming pantos depend very largely for success on:

(1) Characters who will act their parts enthusiastically, exaggerating every movement on stage. Spontaneity is essential in mimed entertainment.

(2) Clear-voiced readers, practised, observant, and intelligent enough to make necessary pauses when audience laughter demands a break.

(3) A few simple but large props. Placards with large printed words can be carried by stage hands in lieu of props, as in early Shakespearian plays. Scene changes are indicated by a placard.

(4) Time for practice.

(5) Good sound effects and P.A. equipment if playing in a large hall.

(6) An imaginative director!

16. Snow White and the Seven Dwarfs

Script by Elspeth Stephenson: directions by Patrick Goodland.

CAST

You will need two readers, and actors for the following parts:
Queen: Very small person
Snow White: The tallest man you can find
Queen No. 2: Evil-looking character
Page: Lanky boy

Any number of people: Dressed up as forest trees made of cardboard, or each simply carrying a placard entitled 'TREE'
Seven Dwarfs—Dressed appropriately
The Prince
Props: A large mirror, made of tinfoil on hardboard. A cardboard Wendy house or house made out of a large box. These can usually be obtained from your local domestic electrical appliance shop; and painted appropriately, with a wide enough aperture for a grown person to put at least his head inside.

SCRIPT

In a turreted castle in falling snow,
The Queen sat down at her window to sew;
(*Queen sitting, holding large-size knitting needles and piece of cloth*)
But as she gazed at the world turned white
A whirling, swirling, dazzling sight—
(*Throw in torn newspaper from the wings*)
She pricked her finger—'Ouch', she cried
And royal blood dropped down outside.
(*Tomato sauce in a thin plastic bag is burst by Queen*)
Mesmerised by the white and the red,
'I wish my daughter these colours,' she said,
'With skin as white as the fleecy snow
And lips as red as my blood below.'

The royal prophecy came true
(*Enter Snow White, who wanders on and straight off the stage*)
Her beautiful daughter, the princess grew
To be called Snow White, but her mother died,
And another Queen graced the King's right side
(*Queen No. 2 sitting at mirror—alternatively someone dressed identically in a frame, who mimes evil Queen's actions*)
This woman was jealous of pretty Snow White,
'I am the most beautiful—it is my right.'
And so a magical mirror she bought,
Sat in her boudoir deep in thought—
'Mirror, mirror on the wall, who is the fairest of us all?'
The mirror replied—'I understand
Thou, Queen, art fairest in the land.'

At that she was glad and with much affection
Repeatedly looked at her reflection.
(*Contortions on the face in the mirror*)
But when a year or so had passed
(*Someone walks across stage with a placard 'YEAR'*)
The Queen looked once again in the glass.
'Mirror, Mirror on the wall
Who is the fairest of us all?'
The mirror spoke truth and told her plain,
'Snow White as queen of beauty doth reign.'
Crash went the mirror—in furious rage
(*Crash of old plates or cymbals off stage*)
She tore out her hair, and screamed to her page
(*Wig hair can be thrown into air*)
'Hither, my boy—your errand is clear—
(*Enter lanky ancient page—looking vacant—sporting an ear trumpet*)
Take Snow White away to the forest and there
Get rid of her quickly—kill her at once
Stop staring stupidly—go on, you dunce.
(*Page adjusts his glasses*)
I am the Queen and you must do my will.
I'll have no rivals—go—Kill, Kill, KILL.'
(*Page faints*)

SCENE 2—if you can BEAR it

(*'Scene 2' placard carried across stage*)
Let's turn aside from this unpleasant Queen
In her splendid palace, to a humbler scene.
'Mid creaking boughs and rustling leaves
(*Appropriate noises off. Trees come on to stage.*)
Little Snow White stands alone and grieves.
(*Enter Snow White with page, who wanders off, leaving Snow White alone*)
In the thick of the wood—yes, alive and kicking,
I think she's all there and her heart's still ticking,
(*Heart effect. Amplified ticking of alarm clock or produce a large alarm clock.*)
For the page couldn't bear to take her life,
And anyway he'd forgotten his knife.

But left to wander, she'd lost her way
(*Snow White wanders back and forth across stage*)
And quite despaired of a place to stay.
But there!—she couldn't believe her eyes—
Stood a trim little house of diminutive size
(*House shuffles on—someone underneath carrying it on, carried unseen by audience*)
'Who on earth could live there?' she exclaimed in delight,
'They couldn't be more than five foot in height!
I'll just go inside and see if it's fit
For a princess to make herself at home in it!'
(*Princess squeezes into house. Some noises as she seeks to occupy. Pause. Trees and house shuffle off. New indoor props brought on stage, or few new placards naming furniture.*)

Placard carried across—SCENE 3

Imagine her now stepping into the dwelling,
Perhaps she was nervous—but then there's no telling.
She'd only been used to fine carpets and plush,
Lavish hangings, chandeliers, velvet—so lush,
But here chairs and table were solid and real
With several places all laid for a meal.
Her tutor at mathematics at the court
She'd bribed to play games—so her knowledge was nought
of countings and numbers—but at a quick guess
She thought there were five, six or seven, no less.
(*Snow White looks at pictures—counts places and then counts on fingers.*)
She gaily explored the bedroom and kitchen.
(*Snow White trips around house*)
'I'd be happy to live here—cooking and stitching—
Court life is so boring, it just made me weep'—
And with that remark she lay down to sleep
On one of the seven beds in a row.
(*Seven people holding 'BED' placard in diminishing height size.*)
(*Placard 'TIME' carried across stage.*)
Time passed, but before you could just say 'Heigh Ho'
A peculiar procession came in from the woods
Of curious creatures in beards and hoods.
(*Enter dwarfs singing 'Heigh Ho! Heigh Ho! Tis home from*

work we go. We work all day and get no pay. Heigh Ho!
Heigh Ho!' Recorded music.)
There was Dopey and Sleepy and all of the rest
Those finest examples of man—English best!
'Hey, brothers,' said Grumpy, 'I sniff a marauder—
Better look 'neath the table and search in the larder.'
What hustling and bustling and hullabaloo!
(A chance for some slapstick).
They hunted around to find out who—
'Oh ho!' said young Happy—'It's Christmas come early'
My present's arrived—a dear little girly!'
(Happy comes forward holding Snow White's hand, while others
act out script.)
As Bashful retreated and Dopey stood staring
Snow White awoke—and got her bearings.
'Oh, darlings,' she said—'What sweeties you are
I'd rather live here than with my false Mama—
Here I shall cook for you, darn all your socks,
My name is Snow White—no, not Goldilocks.'
From then on the cottage was kept spick and span
As Snow White discovered her control over man.
(Snow White runs around with brushes and dusters, making a
great fuss. Some flour on furniture makes plenty of dust.)
There were grumbles and grousing, but all toed the line
And as Sleepy said one day—'We're getting on fine.'

SCENE 4

(Change scenery. Placard 'Silence' carried across stage by
sombre attendant.)
But let us return to Jealousy Hall
Where the Queen reigned nastily over all—
Even the King, I'm sorry to say
—Now there's a result of equal pay!
(Queen looking cruel and cross—mirror again in prominent
position.)
Her magical mirror she picked up one day
Just to be flattered by what it should say.
'Mirror, mirror on the wall,
Who is the fairest of us all?'
(Harsh voice)

'Little Snow White in the forest green
Is far the loveliest, mighty Queen.'
(*Sweet voice.*)
The shock was terrible; her corsets burst.
(*Queen stamps around angrily*)
'This news it's truly the very worst
I've heard,' she said, 'My vengeance dire
I must wreak on that girl—come bring me the attire
Of an old peasant woman—I want a disguise',
(*Page brings on ragged clothes. Queen dresses in them—evil
smile on face.*)
'I'll kill her myself this time to be wise.'
So an old woman crept from the castle gate.
(*Scene changes. Evil Queen walks out, goes round and round
stage between the trees.*)
'I must hurry,' she said, 'before it's too late.'
Her basket of apples looked harmless enough,
(*Basket with apples or coloured balls.*)
But 'neath the gay outside—some poisonous stuff.
(—A moral I see in this visual aid—
But no time to explain while the panto is played)
'Twas easy to find that dear little dwelling
Of the dwarfs and Snow White—the Queen needed no telling.
She knocked at the door and croaked—'Apples for sale—
Red ripe and juicy—I tell you no tale.'
(*Queen knocks on the house which has 'crept' on to the stage.*)
Now 'though Snow White was wary of strangers
This woman could hardly be termed really dangerous.
'Good mother,' she said, 'I'll taste one to try.'
She bit it—alas—and fell down to die.
(*Snow White takes a large bite and collapses. All the trees in
the wood gasped and sighed. Queen dances off—off-stage harsh
chuckles.*)
Or so it appeared to the Queen who then fled,
Chuckling to leave her apparently dead.

When the dwarfs tumbled home they gazed with alarm.
(*Dwarfs stagger around as they look at Snow White.*)
Their capable foreman had come to some harm.
Their beauty, their goddess—'Alas,' said Dopey,
'Now when we come home there'll be no cup of tea.'

There was no doubt about it—the maiden was dead.
(*A dwarf feels Snow White's pulse.*)
And the heart-broken dwarfs, they laid her to bed
In a glass-covered coffin—that all might espy
Her red-and-white beauty as they passed by.
(*Room here for ingenious ideas. Dwarfs parade around Snow White doffing their hats.*)

Now is our tale ended? NO! we can't leave it there.
It remains for the prince to arrive and to stare
(*Enter Prince*)
In wondering rapture, adoring the maid.
'I'll take her—here's money—that beauty won't fade.'
They moved out the coffin—the prince gave a shout!
The piece of the poisonous apple fell out,
(*Enchanted piece of apple clearly marked—large card to resemble apple section. Dwarfs look around through binoculars, or hands over eyes, and run into the audience and pick up some 'fair maidens' who, if possible, have been 'planted'. They then run off with their protesting maids.*)
And life flooded back to the fairest Snow White.
'My prince,' she murmured as he held her tight.
Well, you know what happens, I'll be bound,
And as for the dwarfs—well, they're looking around
For more pretty girls who possibly could
Get lost in that mysterious magical wood!

17. Cinderella

Script by Elspeth Stephenson; Directions by Patrick Goodland.

CAST

Father—Poor man
Cinderella. Small and charming
Two Ugly Sisters. Tall and ugly
Fairy Godmother. Tiny person
Two Heralds
Four Mice/Horses
Two Pages
Any number of Dancers at the Ball
Prince
Script—Suggested actions which can be adapted.

SCENE 1—A kitchen

A man there was in days of yore,
A father, kind, but rather poor,
(*Poorly dressed man walks across the stage.*)
With just one daughter fair and good
Who did exactly what she should.
(*Enter Cinderella, dressed plainly, moving slowly—brushing floor or dusting.*)
Her grace and beauty brought her fame
And Cinderella was her name.
(*Cinderella curtsies and smiles to audience.*)
Her two stepsisters were, however,
Ugly, big and rather clever.
(*Enter sisters, wearing extraordinary clothes.
Exaggerated actions, quarrelling, chasing—generally acting very selfishly. Follow the actions of script.*)
'Cinders, come here, we need more coal.'
'Cinders, this mending, you've left a hole.'
'Cinders, you slut, you lazy wench,
Don't sit there idly on the bench.'
And thus and thus they'd storm and rate
'Til Cinders was in a terrible state.
(*Cinderella rushes around, whirling and dizzy.*)
There came one day an invitiation
To all the ladies of the nation.
(*Enter Heralds—letter received by sisters, who fight over the envelope, which gets torn in the battle!
The envelope should be large, and the invitation gaudy.*)
The king of the country was giving a ball
For Prince Charming, and that wasn't all.
It was at this occasion he'd find him a wife
To love and to cherish the rest of his life.

SCENE 2

The great day came for stepsisters two
(*Sisters dressing hair—Cinderella helping them to prepare for the Ball. Lots of scope in dressing—large hats, wigs, tearing of dresses—using large pins which unfortunately pierce the skins, with much fuss.*)

But not for Cinderella, that wouldn't do.
Cinders helped her sisters dress,
But truth to tell, they looked a mess,
Befrilled and ribboned in gay attire,
To impress the Prince was their desire.
'Be sure,' said one, 'the Prince will fall
In love with me, when we get to the ball.'
(*From one Ugly Sister protrudes large cardboard heart with arrow through it marked U/S to Prince.*)
'Oh, hurry, sister, we'll be late,
The coach is here—come to our fate.'
(*Create scene of real panic: falling and bumping into one another, hats rolling, shoes hurting, etc.*)
So off they swept, no thought to spare
(*Exit Sisters*)
For Cinderella weeping there.
(*Cinderella stands weeping.*)
'It isn't fair, I want to go
But I haven't a dress to wear—and so
(*Cinderella pats her dress, holds up a tattered shawl. Sits on brush.*)
I'll have to sit here all alone.' . . . . . .
She sat there weeping on her own
When suddenly, flash, there in the room
A figure appeared out of the gloom.
(*Photo-flood bulb will give reasonable flash. Fairy appears. Smoke can be produced by powder on a hot plate*)
'Who are you—tell me?' said the maid,
For truth to tell she was afraid.
(*Cinderella looking fearful.*)
'Cinders, Cinders, do not fear,
Your Fairy Godmother is here,
(*Fairy Godmother spreads her hands to the audience.*)
'Tell me what is your request!'
'To go to the ball is what I want best.'
(*Cinderella puts hands to her breast.*)
'And so you shall, my dear, but first
Bring in those garden creatures the worst
And you will see what you will see—
Ha, ha, ha, hee, hee, hee, hee.'
(*Mice enter. Masks should be worn—they come on all fours across the stage. Squeakers off-stage give realism.*)

Imagine now the transformation
From rags to silks—a Paris creation
And the pumpkin, rats and mice of course is
Changed to a handsome coach and horses
(*Cardboard cut to the shape of a coach and horses can be made very simply—they add to the fantasy—the mice have, of course, changed their masks. Cinderella's dress is long and flowing.*)
'Now Cinders,' said this fairy fine,
'Go to the ball but watch the time,
On the last stroke of midnight the magic will end.
(*Cinderella is so excited—dances around the stage.*)
Your silks will be rags—so look, attend.'
'Oh, thank you, thank you, godmother dear.'
said Cinders, and watched her disappear.
She entered the coach which rattled away—
And now comes the next scene in our little play.
(*Cinderella helped in coach from rear—they move off.*)

SCENE 3—At the Ball

The ugly sisters fat and tall
Were there already at the ball.
'I m sure the Prince will dance with me',
'No, sister, you just wait and see—
When he views my lovely face
Across that ballroom he will race—'
(*Smiles—blackened teeth give a loathsome effect.*)
'Huh, that's what you think, no such thing—'
But there we leave them arguing
And to the entrance turn our eyes—
(*Enter Cinderella, escorted by page. Glides gently into the room—several people move back to make room for her entry.*)
To a chorus of 'See' and 'My, My's'
For a radiant figure had appeared
Compared with her, the rest looked weird—
So beautiful she was, so fair
In shimmering silks and satins rare
Little did the sisters guess
That Cinders was this fair princess
But sad they were, and angry, since
They wanted both to wed the prince.

(*Ugly sisters still behaving quite stupidly*.)
(*Enter Prince: follow action of script*.)
Prince Charming gazed at Cinderella
And said to himself—'I'm a lucky fella.'
He knelt before her, kissed her hand,
And danced with her in manner grand.
Thus in gavottes and waltzes gay
They passed the evening hours away.
(*Prince and Cinderella dance. Music—a Viennese Waltz—
should be played off stage*.)
When suddenly—Clang—in solemn chime
The midnight bell tolled out the time.
(*Grandfather clock moves on, someone behind this cardboard
clock can move the hands quickly to midnight*.)
The princess stood stock still and said
'I must away, Goodbye!' and fled.
(*Cinderella and page follow script*.)
'Stop her,' Prince Charming cried—'Oh! wait'—
The place was in uproar, but it was too late.
Such a running and bustling hullabaloo,
Even the herald didn't know what to do
(*Whole cast begins to erupt, rushing, shouting*.)
Everyone murmured, 'Where can she have gone?
What's this? Can it be—the shoe she had on?'
(*Prince finds shoe*.)
'Yes indeed, it's her slipper, a search must begin,
Let everyone help my princess to win.'

SCENE 4

The next morning the herald went out
Along with the Prince (to be sure if in doubt)
(*Herald and Prince go off together. Herald with trumpet in
hand—a page can carry shoe on a cushion*.)
'Hear ye, hear ye, peoples all,
Where'ere you live, in hut or hall,
Every maid must try this shoe
And if it fits—it's the Prince for you.'
(*Sisters waiting, looking in hand mirrors—their feet in bowls
of water. As Prince comes in, there is panic. Follow actions
of script*.)

At last he came to the sisters' dwelling
Both were ready and waiting—they needed no telling
They pushed and pulled and shoved and fought
But their feet were too knobbly, too long or too short.
'Stop, my ladies,' the herald needs cry,
'Leave off, I pray you, you've had your try,
Is there no other lady to try this shoe—
'No, no, 'cept Cinders, and she won't do!
She's only a slut, a kitchen maid!'
'Besides' said the other, 'I'm much afraid
Because of the 'flu, she missed her chance
To shine at the Prince's royal dance.'
'Orders are orders,' the herald declared,
"All must try on the slipper and no one is spared.'

(*Cinderella follows the scripts.*)
Cinderella crept in and tried on the shoe
While her sisters just giggled and said 'She won't do.'
But suddenly one gave a gasp of despair—
(*One of ugly sisters gasps.*)
'It fits,' they all cried, 'Just like that there!'
'At last I've found you,' said the Prince, 'You're mine.
(*Prince takes Cinderella's hand.*)
Bring on the feast, bring on the wine—
(*Pages bring on food or 'goodies' for children in the audience.*)
Let us be married as soon as we may.'
And everyone chorused Hip Hip Hooray.
(*The cast lines up and joins in Hip Hip Hooray.*)

18. The Magic Wood

All actions need to be greatly exaggerated. The humour is in the 'antics' of the players. Well-known club members or leaders generally guarantee an audience response. Imagination and enthusiasm are essential to success.

CAST in order of appearance:

King—a little, tiny person—gaudily dressed
Work-people—poorly dressed
Princess
Fairy—large, tall person, preferably hobnailed boots—
    clumsy

Strong Man—Small, spindly person
Baby Bird—very tall person
Mother Bird—small, short person
Prince—a popular young man
Lion

Props.

Large paint brush, and can marked 'Magic Mousse.'
Large cardboard dish marked 'Princess Pie'
Castle—cut out of large cardboard boxes
Trees of cardboard carried on and off by members of the cast.
    They need to grow! The cast can arrange this simply by
    having a box or form to stand on at the appropriate time.
Axe—Cardboard with a wooden hinged handle will add more
    comedy
Bags of sweets or chocolates

SCRIPT

Once upon a time in a distant land
There lived a king in a castle grand,
(*Suggested actions, which can be adapted: King appears
wearing over-sized crown—surveys his kingdom.*)
He made his people work and slave
But paid no gold for them to save.
(*Enter serfs making very obvious their displeasure and dis-
comfort.*)
Now this old king had a daughter fair,
Just everything she loved to share,
Her clothes, her shoes, her meals and such,
Alas, alack, it wasn't much.
(*Princess gives lots of things—over-sized—to serfs.*)
Now round this castle was a wood,
(*Trees walk on to stage on knees.*)
Where lived a fairy wise and good,
And she decided this old king
Must have a lesson taught to him
With magic brush and paint as well
She quickly cast a magic spell.
(*Fairy replete with wand. Shakes fist at King—paints trees—
lots of room here for slapstick as the 'human' trees are painted.*)
'Trees, trees, grow and grow,
Cover the castle from top to toe,

65

Trees, trees, green and brown
Nobody shall ever chop you down.'
Then all those trees just grew and grew
And hid the castle quite from view.
(*'Trees' grow—players gradually coming to an upright position and stretching up arms.*)
The king then called his people near and said
'To anyone who clears these trees
That hide my castle grand
I'll offer him my daughter's hand!'
(*King has a difficult task getting through trees, who block his way.*)
They came from near, they came from far,
The strongest of the race,
But every time a tree fell down
Another took its place.
(*Enter 'spindly' players. Trees fall as they are felled, but then quickly grow again—much movement at this point.*)

(*Chorus of trees or numerous voices off-stage.*)
'Chop, chop, choppity chop,
Oh dear, what have we got?
These trees never will stop,
Choppity, choppity, chop, chop.'

(*A number of the cast quickly try to grab the axe and try their hand at cutting.*)
Most everybody had a try
But yet the trees were just as high.
(*Princess tiptoes between trees.*)
The princess felt so sad that she
Decided she would go and see.

(*Music*) The wood was very dark and soon
She couldn't see the stars or moon,
And she was almost shedding tears,
(*Princess has a very large handkerchief—a sponge hidden inside can be squeezed over her cheeks as she pretends to wipe away tears.*)
When a faint 'tweet, tweet' came to her ears,

(*Bird enters flapping wings (arms). If possible, Princess sits down and cradles the bird, producing a dummy.*)

A baby bird, too young to fly,
Had fallen from its nest so high.
'The poor wee thing,' the Princess said,
'You've fallen from your little bed.'
She took it in her hand and then
The baby bird was well again.
(*Much commotion as mother bird moves across stage.*)

Suddenly a swishing sound
And Mother Bird flew to the ground.
'You saved the baby I adored,
And you shall have a rich reward.
I know a prince who's brave and true
Who's always been in love with you.
And I will fly to him and say
"Come, take this magic spell away".'
The Mother Bird flew off and then
The Princess was alone again.

(*Lion jumps in making an awful fuss. Chases Princess between trees.*)
Suddenly a lion's roar
Made her frightened all the more.
Out jumped the lion from a wood,
'H-h-h-, this meal looks really good,

(*Large Dish marked 'Princess Pie'*)
A dainty dish, a fair princess
I'll leave just nothing but her dress.'
The Princess stood there filled with fear,
(*Princess trembling.*)
And suddenly came to her ear
(*Princess hand to ear.*)
A tender voice so sweet and clear,
(*Princess smiles.*)
'I will save you, Princess dear,
Begone, cruel lion, on your way
(*Enter Prince—produces sword.*)
There's no meal here for you today.'
His shining sword the lion feared,
(*A light on the blade which can be flashed on is a luxury, not a necessity.*)

He very quickly disappeared
'Oh, thank you, Prince, so brave and true,
What deeds that magic sword can do.
But can you break this magic spell?'
'Don't fear, Princess, all will be well.'
(*Prince puts arm round Princess.*)
The Prince, a path he quickly found
(*Couple go through wood.*)
Which led them home quite safe and sound.
The King was so relieved to see
(*Re-united with King who dances and mumps for joy.*)
His daughter safely back, that he
Proclaimed a public holiday
(*King, hands to mouth.*)
And all good things he gave away (*Music*)
(*King throws sweets to audience. Trees move to sides of stage but still visible.*)
The people filled the banquet hall,
(*People assemble for banquet.*)
The King spoke up to one and all,
'I've been a wicked King, I know
But now I'm old and weary, so
The Prince my daughter he will wed
And he shall be your King instead.
(*These lines to be acted as suggested by the verse.*)
And now I ask the fairy wise
To make the trees their proper size.'
'Good wise fairy of the wood,
Now we have a King who's good,
Please, please, lower the trees
For everything is well,
Take away your magic spell.'
(*Fairy winks to audience.*)

(*Big question mark on card carried across the stage.*)
And can you guess what happened then?
The trees that almost smothered them
Became as small as wood trees should,
(*Trees sink.*)
And that is the end of the Magic Wood. (*Music*).

Curtain.

19. Nelson's last speech

Compere gives a great build-up story about Nelson, the one-eyed admiral and commander. He ends this with the phrase, 'And now, ladies and gentlemen, by turning back the time machine, we are able to bring you one of the most magnificent farewell speeches ever made to his gallant men.'

Nelson, suitably dressed, marches slowly and solemnly on to platform. With a quiet dignity, he surveys the audience, and then, slowly raising his arm, waves his hand as he says 'Ta, Ta', and walks slowly off stage.

20. Larger than life

You will need an extrovert actor who will exaggerate his actions.

Compere. Have you ever thought of ordinary everyday experiences of life as real humour? Think, for instance, of what we look like getting into a seat in a cinema. You come in from a bright sunlit street.

(*Actor enters—squints eyes, gropes with outstretched hands—exaggerated action.*)

C. Why do cinemas have deadly steps?

(*Actor trips, sprawls.*)

C. Getting into the middle seat (that's the one that's usually unoccupied) is like running the gauntlet.

(*Actor moves into imaginary row. Treads on people's toes, stretches across knees—gropes his way to seat and settles, wiping away perspiration from forehead.*)

C. Settling down to enjoy the film, there always seems to be a big head or large hat just in front—or both!

(*Actor simulates movements moving head from side to side, standing up argues with person behind.*)

C. It's amazing how much we eat in the cinema and more especially what we do with wrappers. What trouble-makers they can be!

(*Actor throws sweet paper over head, chews a sweet—chewing noises—continues unwrapping sweets, throwing papers backward over head, surprised when he is thumped by persons behind. He covers his head as blows are rained on him, gets up, begins with speed to sprawl, falls and gets out of the row, running, trips over the stairs, recovers and runs out of the cinema (off-stage.))*

21. The bus queue

You will need two 'ladies' with shopping basket trolleys—eggs, cornflakes, milk and any messy substance. Also a policeman.

Compere. Isn't it amazing what we do with the frustrations of life? For instance, in these days of supermarkets with loaded baskets, two erstwhile friends met one day at a bus stop.

Enter two ladies with loaded trolleys—one bumps into the other—the other retaliates with a bump, then looks the other way. No. 1 then picks out cornflakes out of No. 2's basket, breaks it open, pours it into the trolley. No. 2 slowly yet deliberately takes out bag of flour from No. 1's basket and pours it over her shopping. The fun continues as they each seek to outdo the other. They end up by plastering each other; at the height of the fight, a policeman comes in—gesticulates—he receives same treatment but eventually succeeds in hustling them off to the police station (off-stage.) Large tarts can be made up of crazy foam, and are excellent for spattering over faces of opponents or the policeman.

Variation: In the middle of the fight an innocent party walking by 'receives' a crazy foam pie over his face.

22. Compere, interruptions

To give show-offs a chance to have an audience, and to liven up dinners, dull meetings, etc.!

PUTTING OUT THE FIRE. Someone keeps coming through with a cup of liquid. Finally the leader stops him and says, 'Where's the fire?' He names a local place not in high favour with the group. 'You can't put out that fire with a cup of water.' 'Water? This is kerosene!'

HAVE TO GO FASTER. In full view, someone waves his head and body rhythmically as if he were a pendulum. After a while the leader says, 'What are you doing?' 'I'm keeping time.' 'What time is it?' '4:15.' Leader looks at clock or his watch. 'No, it's five o'clock!' 'Then I'll have to go faster,' says the time-keeper, and does so, swaying more rapidly.

BALONEY. 'We're trying out the acoustics in here.' Leader then calls out, as if calling from one mountain peak to another. 'Baloooooney!' Located in another room, the balcony, or some distant place, his stooge responds: 'Baloooooooney!' In several parts of the room the leader tests with the same result, with the sound louder or softer. Finally, he says, 'Bob Powers* is the best looking guy here!' Echo: 'Baloooooooney!'

23. Three minutes time test

This is a fun paper—a good starter to a social. There is no prize or purpose apart from mixing up the participants and making them vocal. Each person is given the following sheet and everyone must start together—this is important. (You may need to supply each person with a writing instrument. If so, get these ready in advance.)

'CAN YOU FOLLOW DIRECTIONS?
1. Read everything before doing anything.
2. Put your name in the upper right-hand corner of this paper.
3. Circle the word "NAME" in sentence two.
4. Draw five small squares in the upper left-hand corner of this paper.
5. Put an "X" in each square.
6. Sign your name under the title of this paper.
7. Put a circle around sentence five.
8. Put an "X" in the lower left-hand corner of this paper.
9. Draw a triangle around the "X" you just put down.
10. Draw a rectangle around the word "PAPER" in sentence four.
11. Loudly call out your first name when you get to this point.
12. If you think you have followed directions carefully to this point, call out "I have."
13. On the reverse side of this paper add 8950 and 9850.
14. Put a circle around your answer and a square around the circle.
15. Count out in a normal speaking voice, from 10 to 1 backwards.
16. Punch three small holes in the top of this paper with your pencil point.

* Use the name of a well-known person in the audience.

17. If you are the first person to reach this point, call out loudly, "I AM THE FIRST PERSON TO REACH THIS POINT, AND I AM THE LEADER IN FOLLOWING DIRECTIONS."
18. Underline all the even numbers on this side of the paper.
19. Say out loudly, "I AM NEARLY FINISHED AND I HAVE FOLLOWED DIRECTIONS."
20. Now that you have finished reading carefully, do only sentence two.'

24. The match game

An ice breaker or social starter. Each person is given the following paper. A specified time is allowed for answering the questions. The papers are then collected, and a reader selects a number which are read individually. When a paper has been read, the MC suggests the names of some people in the audience whose paper it might be. The volume of applause is taken as an indication of whether the MC is likely to be right or wrong. Here is the paper:

INSTRUCTIONS

Please answer the questions below, filling in the blanks. As your answer, give the first thought that comes to your mind! Don't spend any time thinking about it.
1. For my favourite dessert I would select................................
2. I would like to go on holiday to................................
3. In my pocket my ....contains my money.
4. If I could choose what car I wanted to own, I would choose a................................
5. In my home the ....are at the top of the staircase.
6. Last year I was................................more than once.
7. I have................ hair,................ eyes and a................................
8. In my living room I have................................curtains.
9. When I came home, I was told there was a................in the oven.
10. Although I like to read, I do not always enjoy................................
11. I often................................in front of the television.
12. I have a sweet tooth and wish that................................was always on the menu.

13. Although it was a dark night the...................shone brightly.
14. ....was all over the road after the accident.
15. I spend time in the garden to................................flowers.
16. Bath night is on...........................night.

25. London Underground and Railway Stations

A party starts. Participants are given a sheet with the clues for names of London stations. They are allotted a certain time to complete the answers.

1. Egg-shaped ....
2. Dark Monks ....
3. Home of Moriarty's enemy ....
4. Continental retreat ....
5. Top people's open space ....
6. What a holy man uses for bowling ....
7. Do rabbits live here? ....
8. Where you lose your head ....
9. Coloured river crossing ....
10. The disconsolate widow ....
11. Priest's field ....
12. Place for spreading the Good News ....
13. Sounds as if a football team captured the street ....
14. Won on the playing fields of Eton ....
15. Canine cries ....
16. John O'Gaunt's Portal ....
17. Shakespeare country ....
18. Royal Road ....
19. Leave your money here ....
20. 1,760 yards gone ....
21. Rough seas do this to some people ....
22. This dyke needs supporting ....
23. Burial place for sappers ....
24. No gate across this lane ....

(Answers, see Appendix C)

26. The book game

Another social starter. Titles and authors are written on separate cards, placed around the hall or home. Players have paper and pencil and have to match the book title with the author's name. The first person to complete all the series is the winner. Here are some suggestions to give you the idea but it would be more fun to improve on them and make up your own.

Swollen Rivers—Lettice Wade (Example: Let us wade)
No Vintage Year—M. T. Sellars
Wonderful Eyes—C. Allways
The Drowning Damsel—Ada Boyes
Maiden in Danger—O. Warner
English Summer—O. Howitt Raynes (O how it rains)
Climbing in Lake Land—I. Gasper Bitte (I gasp a bit)
Brilliant Future—Rosie Hughes
Stammering Samuel—Wattis E. Saye (What does he say)
A Wife in Hiding—Betty Covering
The Hungry Years—Norah Crust
Henpecked—Olive Mealone.

27. A real hoot

Props: Six large cards about 14 in. × 8 in., on which the following words are printed: Coffee, cheese and biscuits; sweet; meat and veg; fish; soup.

The story-teller relates how a man fell asleep, having dined well in a restaurant car. The food caused him to have a nightmarish dream. He was taking his meal backwards. He gets mixed up with the rhythm and noise of the train.

Holding up the 'Coffee card, the leader starts:

COFF-EE;   COFF-EE;   COFF-EE

the two syllables begin fairly slowly as the imaginary train pulls out of the station. As the audience joins in, so the card 'cheese and biscuits' appears, and the train's rhythm moves a little faster.

CHEESE AND BISCUITS: CHEESE AND BISCUITS

next: SWEET: SWEET: SWEET

—said fairly quickly, with a short pause between each utterance as the rhythm picks up

then: MEAT & VEG: MEAT & VEG: MEAT & VEG:

this to be repeated quickly with short pauses.

The train is now really moving and the card 'fish' appears:

FISH: FISH: FISH: FISH:

—increasing the speed so that the audience can just get the word out.

Suddenly the train approaches a road signal light.
The card 'soup' is held up, and everyone cries in a high pitched voice:

SOOOOOOOOOOOOP

as the train comes to a halt.

Variation
Divide the audience into sections, starting one off and then another, but eventually all ending with 'soup' together. For this you need extra leaders and extra cards according to the number of groups.

28. Fun songs

'Oh, not another verse!' Camp and concert songs can be a bore and even disagreeable, if they are long-winded and repeated too often. We've known situations where the M.C.'s 'just once again' has aroused audible moans.

But there is positive value in singing—if used with discretion. It encourages involvement and relaxation.

Nonsense and community singing requires leadership (preferably by someone who is not tone deaf!) Words can be illuminated on a screen, written boldly on card or the back of wallpaper. Use at least two-inch letters.

There is a mountain of traditional and modern material available.

The following nonsense songs are more enjoyable if suitable actions are worked out, and if the leader exaggerates the actions up front.

A. THE CHESTNUT TREE

The verse is sung and acted over and over again. With each repetition, a fresh word is replaced by an action, until all the words are taken out. The pianist plays regularly throughout, keeping time and rhythm. Finally, all sing the complete song at a faster speed.

1. Under the spreading chestnut tree,
   Where I held you on my knee,
   I kissed you and you kissed me,
   Under the spreading chestnut tree.

2. Under the (*omit word and spread both arms sideways*) chestnut tree, etc. (*Treat last line as first.*)
3. Under the (*as 2—and strike chest with both hands*) -nut tree, etc.
4. Under the (*as in 2 and 3—and touch forehead with both hands*) tree, etc.
5. Under the (*as in 2, 3 and 4—and raise both arms, fingers extended*), etc.
6. (*Stoop, with hands towards floor*) the (*as in 2, 3, 4, 5*), etc.
7. (*as in 1, 2, 3, 4, 5, 6*), Where I (*clasp arms across chest*) you on my knee, etc.
8. (*as in 1, 2, 3, 4, 5, 6*), Where I (*as in 7*) on my (*slap knees*) etc.
9. (*as in 1, 2, 3, 4, 5, 6*), (*as in 8*), (*Point to self*) kissed you, and you kissed (*point to self*).
10. (*as in 1, 2, 3, 4, 5, 6*), (*as in 8*), (*as in 9*) kissed (*point to someone else*), and (*point to someone else*) kissed (*as in 9*).

11. (as in 1, 2, 3, 4, 5, 6), (as in 8), (as in 10) but make noise
    with lips.

B. WOAD

(Tune: *Men of Harlech*)

What's the use of wearing braces,
Vests and pants, and shoes with laces,
Ties and things you buy in places,
    Down the old High Road?
What's the use of shirts in nylon,
Knitwear with the latest style on,
Agonies they simply pile on,
    Better far is Woad.

Woad's the stuff to show men,
Woad to scare your foemen,
Boil it to a brilliant hue,
Rub it on your back and your abdomen,
Ancient Briton never hit on,
Anything as good as Woad to fit on,
Neck or knees, or where you sit on,
    Tailors you be blowed!

C. THE CROCODILE SONG

She sailed away on a lovely summer's day
    on the back of a crocodile.
'You see,' said she, 'He's as tame as tame can be,
    I'll ride him down the Nile'.
The croc. winked his eye, as the lady waved goodbye,
    Wearing a happy smile.
At the end of the ride the lady was inside
    and the smile was on the crocodile.

D. SAUSAGE SONG

SAUSAGE SONG

There are lots and lots of
  things that I should like
  to know.
Such as what is II R3 and
  how do winkles grow.
How to cube a beetroot,
How to stop a leak,
But there's just is one question
  that I couldn't answer in
  a week.

Chorus:

What was the sausage like
  before it had its skin?
Was it short and tubby,
  was it long and thin?
Did it have to have one to
  keep the gravy in?
What was the sausage like
  before it had a skin?

E. FAR AWAY

(Tune: *Marche Militaire—Schubert*)

Far, far away in a small town in Germany
There lived a toymaker, Schubert was his name
Ish man musica, ish man speiler, ish man musica

1. Ish man viola . . . Vio-vio-viola (repeat 3 times)
    Far, far away, etc.
2. Ish man banjo . . . Plunkity, plunkity, plunk, plunk, plunk
       (Repeat 3 times + viola)
    Far, far away, etc.
3. Ish man drummer . . . Bompity, bompity, bom, bom, bom
       (Repeat 3 times + 1 and 2)
    Far, far away, etc.
4. Ish man trombone . . . Umpah, umpah, umpa-pah
       (Repeat 3 times + 1, 2 and 3)
    Far, far away, etc.
5. Ish man bagpipes . . . (repeat all instruments)

Chapter 5

Ideas for Celebrating Christmas

The annual celebration of Christmas can be a time when people recognize the joy of remembering the Saviour's birth and begin to see some of its implications. Many Christmas customs have been handed down to us, but in essence, Christmas is (rightly) a time of giving, peace and goodwill. Christmas celebrations can amplify the real significance of this Christian festival.

To help celebrate Christmas in a community, we offer the following ideas. Some arise from long-standing traditions, and many can have almost infinite variations.

1. Carolling

Youth groups, clubs, choirs and bands often use this time for collecting for the less fortunate people of the world. Official carol parties need to be registered by the charity for which they are collecting. Most organizations can give their own supporters an immense amount of help, often to supplying carol sheets, boxes, etc. Institutions need to be alerted about proposed visits. Hospitals and homes often welcome a group, so long as prior notice has been given. Friendships can be developed if at the end of each evening and in different homes, the party is able to share in simple refreshments. A small present given to lonely people can bring a great sense of cheer. Cards indicating that a carol party is to visit a particular location will usually add extra interest—and money for the collecting box.

Carol sheets, visitation material and boxes are readily available from many charity organizations.

2. Carol concerts

Traditional carol concerts are still very popular in our own country. They can be used by church groups as a means of presenting the essential Christmas message of love, joy and peace to many who may have lost touch with what Christmas is really all about. A well-practised group of singers and a good leader are, of course, essential. Informality is a great asset. Some of the traditional Christmas songs—Good King Wenceslas, The Twelve Days of Christmas, etc.—can be used in the first half of the programme, together with readings from Dicken's *Christmas Carol* and other items which can either be read by one person, or a group, or acted. Items should be short in duration, variety being the aim. Various groups within any organization could be invited to offer items for the programme. Some of the customs of Christmas could be explained, with suitable illustrations, e.g. the decorated Christmas tree, whose origin can be traced to about 1460 in Germany. The lighted Christmas tree is credited to Martin Luther who lived from 1483 to 1546. Understanding the origin of the plum pudding, the turkey, the star, the fruit cake, together with many other traditions, can bring a new significance to Christmas.

Hot coffee and mince pies served half-way through a carol concert can stimulate friendship and conversation.

The second half of the programme could consist of the more Christian carols directly related to the events recorded in the Bible, and an epilogue, including nativity play, film, slides and a reading, can bring the evening to a meaningful conclusion.

Information on Christmas traditions is readily available at most libraries—see Appendix for suggestions.

3. Carol services

These should be planned well in advance, and each item and reading well practised. There is nothing worse than sitting through a service where readers cannot be heard. This service can be based upon the traditional nine lessons and carols, or can be developed along more informal lines. Good music retail stores or church suppliers usually supply samples on request and Novellos of Sevenoaks, Kent, often loan demonstration tapes or cassettes to would-be customers.

4. Christmas morning family services

The popularity of these gatherings in many suburban churches is perhaps evidence of their value. The emphasis in the invitation should always be on the family. Children can be encouraged to bring with them the favourite present which they have been given. It is terribly hard for them to be separated from a cuddly teddy bear or a moon rocket which they have just received.

Remember that many of the Mums and Dads will have been up early. So why not allow a number of the carols to be sung seated? The timing of such a service is important: an early start has been found suitable in many areas. The children have probably been up since crack of dawn anyway, and an early start also gives Mum time to get home to oversee the cooking of the Christmas meal. Some of the new presents received by the children may make effective visual aids for a short address. Experience has shown that three-quarters of an hour is an ideal time for this service to last. Coffee served after the service enables individuals to greet one another. A retiring offering, for refugees or for a charity which helps the underprivileged, is appropriate.

5. Christmas publicity

There are many good pre-printed cards and leaflets available —for example, from the Christian Publicity Organization, Ivy Arch Road, Worthing, Sussex. This inexpensive form of publicity can be taken personally to families with the greetings of the church or organization. The leaflets should be distributed in good time, so that families can plan their arrangements.

6. Christmas decorations

The use of greenery at Christmas has grown out of ancient Roman and Greek customs. Christians have adopted these customs, especially the holly, the blood-red berries symbolizing the piercing thorns which were placed upon our Saviour's brow. Evergreens, pine cones, sprayed with appropriate lacquers, artificial poinsettia and other suitable materials,

83

make ideal home and hall decorations. Candles made out of cardboard, decorated with red paper, with an electric candle bulb placed in a hoop surrounded by evergreen leaves, make effective illuminations for Carols by Candlelight services. Aim at simplicity and yet quality. Many commercial firms willingly pass on their Christmas decorations, window dressings etc. after the Christmas celebrations. If these are carefully stored, they can be adapted for use the following year.

7. Decorating churches

Someone with an artistic eye should be given the overall responsibility, but a particular family or group can find new depths of friendship by being given this task. Give the congregation ample warning of the materials required, and you will usually find the whole operation is inexpensive. Encourage artistic members to plan this activity, but always safeguard yourself by reserving the power tactfully to veto schemes or make adjustments.

8. Group decoration parties

Youth groups and Sunday School classes can be encouraged to make appropriate decorations as a surprise Christmas present for their parents. This can be done in the weeks prior to Christmas. Lanterns, bells, a nativity scene, Christmas tree decorations, Christmas table decorations and paper craft items are always very acceptable, and parents are usually delighted with their surprise gift. Groups may like to consider donating some decorations to the local hospital wards, such as a Christmas decoration for each bedside table. This needs to be negotiated with the Ward Sister. Senior Citizens' homes and geriatric wards are often very glad of this help.

9. Viewing City and Town illuminations

Why not take the house-bound senior citizens—or other less fortunate people—on a tour round your local decorations, returning to a home or hall for refreshments?

10. Christmas Parties (For games, see *Games Galore*, also published by Scripture Union.)

For children under ten, aim at simplicity, and avoid games where individual losers are counted out early in the game.

Elevens to fourteens require a lot of activity. Noise and bustle will assure the success of a party for this age-group. The group can be encouraged to decorate the venue. (See ideas for theme parties.)

Games for adults need to be carefully selected so that no one is exhausted after the first few games. Wall competitions, sitting-down games and entertainment are usually appreciated.

For a youth group, half the pleasure of a party is in looking forward to it. A committee should draw up the suggestions, and areas of responsibility should be given to members of the committee or other people within the group. It is often useful to hand round a questionnaire before any decision are made. The following will enable all members of the group to express themselves and can lead to greater participation in the effort:

Activity	*Enthusiastic*	*Possible*	*Definitely No*
Fancy Dress			
Sit-down meal			
Table games			
Mini sports			
Party games			
Entertainment			
Theme party			
Films			
Conjuring			
Illus. Travel			
Talk			
Music			
etc.			

11. Theme parties

A. Ship's party

The hall is decorated as a ship. Make circular portholes with a fish or a whale looking in, and then pin these on to the curtains or place over the windows. A simple bridge can be constructed. Life belts can be made out of old rubber tyres wrapped round with white cloth, and painted white and decorated with the name of the ship. All the games should be given a nautical flavour. A gang-planks entrance through a darkened area can always be an effective introduction. Nets (garden) can be hung up with artificial fish dangling. Lighting effects can be made out of old lanterns. Songs, hymns and the epilogue theme can be about the sea.

B. Pirates' party

The hall is suitably decorated as pirate ship or else as a darkened pirate's cave. Crew should be dressed appropriately —eye patches, dusters for head-dresses and over-sized earrings with coloured clothing. Encourage as many of the guests as possible to dress up. Out of the treasure chest all sorts of interesting things can appear, e.g. games apparatus, prizes, and (depending on size) 'booty' and even the captain's wife. Sea shanties and weirdie music on tape would be suitable background accompaniment.

C. Gipsy party

For a smallish number the hall can be decorated as a caravan or for a larger groups as a gipsy camp with an artificial fire, stewpot, etc. Gipsy background music should accompany the evening and the menu should have a gipsy flavour.

D. Other suggestions Tramps Nursery Rhymes Beatrix Potter stories

Many other themes will suggest themselves to party organizers. Aim at simplicity, good organization, suitable refreshments and novelty.

(For Christmas Drama, see pp. 94–109)

12. Christmas parcels for the lonely

If you are unaware of people in need, call in on your local social services office, outlining what the group or organization is prepared to offer. This will usually produce lists of carefully selected and really needy folk. Preparation for this project must be put in hand soon after the summer holidays.

A box for the collection of goods in kind or cash should be available at most group gatherings for several weeks. A poster outlining the particular kind of contents is essential—old ladies don't usually appreciate a pair of sheer nylon tights! Ask older acquaintances what kind of ingredients they would enjoy receiving.

If young people undertake the delivery, you should deliver letters, saying what you intend to do, before the actual distribution takes place. Doors are much more likely to be opened during the day than on a dark evening. You should also give some instruction about how to approach older members of the community, otherwise young people may find it difficult to handle genuine fear, bordering on mistrust. Distributors should introduce themselves in a friendly, bright, but not boisterous way. They should explain immediately who they are, and should speak clearly. This will give them confidence, and give confidence also to the old people they are visiting.

13. Christmas meals for the lonely or senior citizens

(See Chapter 7, Section 6.)

14. Candle creations

Numerous do-it-yourself shops sell utensils and materials for making decorative candles. Younger groups need careful supervision but this fascinating art is useful and remunerative for many youth groups.

15. Christmas cards for the elderly and shut-ins

A 'meals on wheels' visitor congratulated an old lady on the number of Christmas cards she had received—about twenty, all along the mantelpiece. Rather sadly, she replied, 'No, dear, I haven't had a Christmas card sent to me for many years now. These are old ones which I bring out every year. It makes it look a bit Christmassy, doesn't it?' (Quoted in *Yours* No. 3, Nov. 1973)

A card or small gift can bring a sense of belonging and the knowledge of concern. Preparation of lists of lonely or older people should begin soon after the summer is over. Why not get together with several friends to draw up a list of lonely people which you all share? Then you can arrange to deliver cards to people on the list on different days leading up to Christmas.

Chapter 6

Short Plays with Christian Themes

Drama brings involvement, creativity and friendship into a group. A play needs not only actors but also a supporting team, so the teenager who would not be seen dead on the stage finds his niche among the backroom boys. The director needs to stress the interdependence of each member of the group in this activity and to be sensitive to the talents and ability of his team. Drama can also involve parents in making costumes and props, etc. All the scripts included here have been successfully used. Most of them were written for a North London surburban community. They can be adapted freely. Some of them were born and (to change the metaphor) hammered out in group discussions. It is my hope that many youth groups will use their creative abilities and modern insights to write and produce thought-provoking drama.

1. Paul's escape from Damascus

There is no greater Christian character and exponent of the Christian way than Paul the great Apostle.

CAST

Narrator	Ananias
First Traveller	James
Second Traveller	Martha
Citizen	Elizabeth
First Pharisee	Third Traveller
Second Pharisee	Fourth Traveller
Paul	First Guard
Centurion	Second Guard
Judas	

There can be other Citizens who do not have speaking parts.

Narrator: A man named Saul had set out for Damascus, intent on persecuting the young church in that town. But as he travelled, the Lord Jesus Himself met Saul on the way, and Saul immediately realized his own need of a Saviour. After being visited by Ananias in Damascus, he was befriended by the group of Christians, and was to be found every day, telling of the wonderful thing that had happened to him. Saul became known as Paul, and became Paul the great Apostle. However, the Pharisees, his former friends, were increasing in their hatred and opposition to him, as we shall see.

Our first scene is the market place at Damascus.

SCENE 1—Market Place.

Some citizens going to and fro. Two travellers enter, and stop a passer-by.

1st Trav. Excuse me, Sir.

Citizen: Yes?

1sr Trav.: We are looking for Paul.

2nd Trav.: We have come from our village to hear him tell the good news of Jesus Christ.

Citizen: Oh, *that* Paul. He's a strange one. No one here understands him. He comes to the market place most mornings; if you go that way, you may meet him coming down.

1st Trav.: Let's go!

2nd Trav.: (*as they hurry away*): Thank you very much.
(*Exit Travellers; enter two Pharisees*)

1st Phar.: Hey, you!

Citizen: Me?

1st Phar.: Who else? Is that fellow Paul coming here again this morning?

Citizen: Yes. They say that. . . .

1st Phar.: Quiet! Away with you. (*Exit citizen*)

2nd Phar.: How much longer can we put up with this? Huge crowds come to listen, and some of the leading Jews are becoming followers of this Jesus?

1st Phar.: We Pharisees must do something.

2nd Phar.: What about the Roman guard? We might get Paul arrested.

1st Phar.: That's an idea—you can stay and stir up the crowd; I'll go and get the guard.
(*Exit 1st Phar. Enter Paul with Citizens, travellers, etc.*)

Paul: Now friends, we have come again to proclaim the good news of Jesus Christ, who was sent from God to die for us, and who rose again and lives with God—

2nd Phar. (*interrupting*):   How could He rise from the dead? (*He is ignored*).

Paul: You all know how I hated Jesus, and hunted His followers. I, too, thought He was dead, until He met me on the road to Damascus. Then there was no doubt. I had to leave my old ways and follow him.

2nd Phar.:   You have betrayed your countrymen and your religion, Paul.

2nd Citizen: Let Paul speak.

All: Yes, let him speak.

2nd Phar. (*trying to make himself heard*):   We, too, should be heard.

All (*impetuously*):   Quiet, you; we have come to hear Paul. (*There follows a brief uproar. Enter centurion, with members of guard*)

Cent.:   Silence here! Or you will be arrested. Which one is Paul? (*Hubbub on all sides. Crowds close around Paul*)

Cent.:   Make way! Which one of you is Paul?

Paul (*coming to front of crowd*):   I am he.

Cent.:   It is said that each day you bring uproar to the market place.

Paul: I have permission to address the townsfolk here. The uproar was not my doing.

Judas: That's true. It was that fellow there who started it all (*points at 2nd Pharisee*)

All: That's right, it was him. (*1st Pharisee exchanges angry words with his colleague*)

Cent.:   Well, that's as may be. This is your last warning. Now break up and go to your homes. (*Crowd and guards leave. Only Pharisees are left*)

1st Phar.:   There is nothing for it. We will have to kill him. And it should be tonight. (*They leave.*)

SCENE 2

Narrator: Later that same day Paul returned to the house of his friend Judas, in the street called Straight, where he had lived during his stay in Damascus. Together they discuss the day's events.

(*This scene takes place in Judas' room, lit by a candle. Judas paces to and fro while Paul is seated.*)

Judas: I am afraid there will be trouble after today. Those Pharisees looked very angry.

Paul: Yes. There is no doubt that their hearts are turned against the Lord Jesus. But I am sure He will provide for us.

Judas: Perhaps you should leave the city for a while.

(*An urgent knock on the door*)

Judas: Who's there?

Anan.: Ananias.

Judas: Come in.

(*Ananias enters, breathless*)

Anan.: Paul, listen; this is important. We have heard that the Pharisees are plotting to kill you.

Paul: Are you sure of this?

Anan.: Yes, a friend has told us it is already decided.

(*Another knock, and James enters quickly*)

James: Half the city is out looking for you, Paul. They are alreading searching in twos and threes, and have sworn to kill you.

(*Enter Martha and Elizabeth*)

Martha: Paul, we have just heard the Roman guard are looking for you, too.

Eliz.: Yes, they have been persuaded that you must be arrested at once.

(*A tramping is heard outside, with Centurion calling orders, e.g. 'left, right, left, right, right wheel,' etc.*)

James (*hearing the soldiers outside*): Quick, put out the light.

(*Ananias puts it out. James and Judas watch at window*)

Judas: They are going by.

Anan.: Paul, we must get you out at once. You can leave from my house on the wall. James, can you distract the guard at the gate?

James: Yes—I think so.

Eliz.: We will prepare some food for the journey.

Paul: I shall be very sad to leave, but it would seem to be for the best. I shall go to Jerusalem.

Anan.: Let us go and get ready.

(*They all leave*)

SCENE 3

Narrator: Within a short time they had gathered at the house of Ananias. Meanwhile the search within the city continued, and guards were posted at every gate to keep an eye on travellers and watch for Paul.

Scene 3 takes place by a small gate in the city wall.

(*Two guards are on duty. Enter two travellers*)

1st Guard (brandishing spear): Halt! Who is there?

3rd Trav.: Two travellers from the country, to visit friends.

4th Trav.: Why are we stopped like criminals?

2nd Guard: We are looking for Paul, who must be arrested at all costs.

4th Trav.: May we go on our way?

1st Guard: Yes, but go carefully.

(*They go into the city*)

(*Enter James, from the city, at a run*)

1st Guard: Stop! Who are you?

James: Are you looking for Paul?

2nd Guard: Yes; do you know where he is?

James: Come with me quickly.

1st Guard: We must not leave the gate.

James: There is promotion in this for whoever catches Paul.

(*The guards look at each other. One makes up his mind.*)

2nd Guard: I'm going. No one will come by this gate.

(*They both leave, following James. A group of Christians with Paul now appear either (a) at a window in the wall, or (b) on top of the wall. This depends on the ease of organizing a basket!*)

Anan.: I think they have gone.

Judas: James will have them half-way to the city square by now.

Eliz.: Half way to the city prison, if you ask me.

Paul: I had better be going. Take courage, knowing that the work of the Lord Jesus will continue, and that He will be with you constantly. Nothing can separate us from Him and His love. Now I must thank you all for your Christian love and kindness.

Martha: Do you have all you need?

Paul: Yes, thank you. It is all here in my pack.

(*They prepare to let Paul down. He reaches ground safely.*)

Anan.: God-speed, Paul. Perhaps we shall meet in Jerusalem.
All: Farewell, farewell, Paul.
Narrator: And so Paul, though he was sorry to do so, left his friends and travelled on with the good news, being sure that the Lord had still a great deal for him to do.

2. A Christmas Pageant

A play for children—by Elspeth Stephenson

CAST

Sally
Bruce
Father Christmas, with several small children
Group of carol singers
Cook, maid and children
A few shepherds
Three Wise Men (or Kings)

Scene—An ordinary living room in a modern-day house
Music—taped, records and/or piano

Sally is sitting alone at the table, sighing and frowning over the homework books spread out before her.
Sally: Well—that's the history done. Now, what next . . . Oh, yes—
  (*Enter Bruce with two mugs of steaming cocoa*)
Bruce: Mum says you're to finish soon 'cos it's nearly bedtime. Here you are! (*Hands over mug*)
Sally: Finish? I haven't even started my English. Suppose Mum's watching tele!
Bruce: Yep.
Sally: Wish I could. Fancy giving us homework in the last week of term.
Bruce: S'pose it is a bit thick—'though if you will go to such a soppy school . . .
Sally (*flying into a rage*): Ooh—do you want cocoa all over you or—
Bruce (*interrupting*): Keep your hair on, Sal—what is it anyway?
Sally: Well it's composition. Miss Pritchard's given us the title.

Bruce: Let's see (*leans over, grabs rough book and reads*) 'Imagine you have a friend who has never heard of Christmas. Explain to him what it's all about.' Cor!— well, he'd be a bit of a dim-wit, if he'd never heard of Christmas.

Sally: Now don't be awkward, you know what she means.

Bruce: All right. Now try it on me.

Sally: What?

Bruce (*standing with arms folded*): I don't know what Christmas is all about. Tell me!

Sally: Christmas is a time of—it's when all the family get together, and oh, this is stupid. I can't do it on you— because I know you know, and you know I know you— Oh—

Bruce: Try another way. Put down all the things you can think of to do with Christmas.

Sally: O.K. Let's start a clean page. (*They sit down together.*) There's holly, and mistletoe and crackers and games and . . .
(*During this sentence, the lights dim, 'Jingle Bells' music begins faintly, getting louder as Father Christmas, carrying a sack, and surrounded by lots of clamouring children, 'Please, I want a doll . . . is there something for me . . . when can we look' . . . and similar remarks, walks up aisle from back of hall—spotlighted if possible.*)

Bruce (*while Santa is half-way down hall*): Why, look! It's Father Christmas.

Sally: Santa Claus! He's important at Christmas. I'll put him down. (*writes*)

Santa: Thank you, Sally, I'm glad I'm not forgotten. But remember, there's more to Christmas than stockings full of toys.
(*Santa and children group at back on one side*)

Sally: I will, thanks a lot for coming. Oh dear, now I'm stuck again.

Bruce: Let's think what we do on Christmas Day. There's circus on the television.

Sally: And the Queen's speech. And party games. (*Group of Carol singers in coats, scarves etc., one holding a lantern, music book etc. walk slowly up the aisle, singing carol.*)

Sally: Look what's coming—carol singers!

(*The carol singers finish their carol, moving to group at the back on the other side*)

Bruce: That was great. Just like on a Christmas card.

1st Carol Singer: But don't forget what we were singing about.

Bruce: Singing about—oh, about the baby and everything. Well, we all know you're singing about Christmas, or it wouldn't be a carol, would it?

Sally: We don't want to get all religious—Oh, look out, yes, this is more like it.

(*Enter chef or cook, bearing Christmas pudding, with waitress carrying sauce boat, followed by a few children gleefully clashing spoons and forks to the tune of—either 'We wish you a merry Christmas' or 'Food, glorious food.'*)

Sally (*when they reach the top*): Oh—I'm glad you've come— food and lots of it at Christmas.

(*She writes*)

Cook: Yes, indeed—and here's a slice for each of you. (*Cuts pudding and hands slices over.*) But don't forget the child whose parents couldn't even buy a night's lodging. He knew what hunger was, I'll be bound.

Bruce: You know, it's odd, these characters (*retreats to group at back*) keep giving us snatches of advice.

Sally: Don't bother them—just enjoy it! (*with mouth full*) I didn't know that we got free refreshments an' all.

Bruce (*eating*): Mm—Mm

(*A few shepherds have entered from behind the children. One taps Sally on the shoulder.*)

Sally: Stop nudging me, Bruce.

Bruce: I didn't.

(*Shepherd taps her again*)

Sally: There you go again. (*Looks round and jumps up.*)

Sally: Oh! sorry, sire—I didn't see you were there.

1st Shepherd: That's all right. We've just come as a reminder. Don't forget the star. (*He looks back and points up to where a star is now shining. Sally, Bruce and all on the stage look up, too. While they are looking, three wise men enter from rear down the aisle bearing gifts, to music of 'We Three Kings.' When half way down, Sally turns and nudges Bruce—*)

Sally: Look!

Bruce: Crumbs. We've got royalty coming. Did you get the shepherds down?

Sally: No, I'll just do it. (*writes*)

Bruce: Say, Sal, how do you address a king—sir, or—

Sally (*whispers*):   Your majesty, I think.
(*Three kings arrive*)

Bruce: Welcome, your majesties.

1st King: We thank you—(*pause*) but do you welcome the child we go to worship?
(*They move on to the back, kneeling towards the star, opposite the shepherds.*)

Sally: Whew! I'm glad they've gone.

Bruce: Read out what you've got so far.

Sally: At Christmas we always have Santa Claus who brings children presents. There are carol singers and lots of food always—

Bruce: That doesn't sound right.

Sally: Be quiet! (reads) 'Lots of food always, shepherds and wise men.'

All other characters together: But you have forgotten some-one.

Bruce (*looking round uneasily*):   Don't you mean something?

Santa: No—we give presents at Christmas because 'God so loved the world that He gave His Son.'

Cook: We enjoy ourselves at this time, for the angel said 'I bring good news for you—this very night in David's town your Saviour was born—Christ the Lord.'

1st Carol Singer: We sing because this is the most wonderful thing that has ever happened.

Sally: But excuse me a minute—all this is a lovely story, but does it make any difference today?

1st Shepherd: We went to Bethlehem to see all this, not because a good child had been born—but because God Himself had become man.

1st King: This man, Jesus, came to show God's love—

2nd King: He came to tell of God's forgiveness—

3rd King: He came to give new life.

All: And he still does this today.
(*All except Sally and Bruce process off to a carol, and music continues very faintly while Sally and Bruce are left.*)

Bruce: I think you've got quite a lot more to write.

Sally (slowly): I know—and I don't quite understand it all.

Bruce: Well, let's go and talk it over with Mummy.

Sally: But it's your favourite T.V. programme on in a few minutes.

Bruce: Oh, I can miss it just for once. This is much more important. Come on.

(Exit Sally and Bruce. Music swells up.)

3. Emmanuel—God with us

A Nativity play based on two poems—'The Inn that missed its chance' by Amos R. Wells, and 'The Journey of the Magi' by T. S. Eliot, whose poems are published by Faber and Faber. Adapted by Patrick Goodland.

This can either be performed without a set on an empty stage, leaving the audience to imagine the various scenes, or by providing a simple divided set.

The Set: Front of an eastern inn, low doorway through which the Innkeeper can appear and the other characters enter. This should be set at an angle to the audience.

Introduction: Recorded music.

Narrator (Spotlighted): Christmas is a time of joy and happiness. The strange, impressive, colourful pageantry of our western celebrations may eclipse the simplicity and beauty of the Divine drama which took place nearly 2,000 years ago in the insignificant town of Bethlehem. Mistakes are common to humans; how could the Innkeeper have known that the weary Mary, expecting her first-born, and her faithful Joseph, were being chosen and honoured by God to bring His only Son into this world?

Innkeeper (The innkeeper performs this outside the inn door. As the spotlight moves from narrator to keeper, he speaks as though he is conversing with a crowd of visitors):
What could be done? The Inn was full of folk;
His Honour, Marcus Lucius, and his scribes
Who made the census; honourable men
From farthest Galilee came hitherward
To be enrolled; high ladies and their lords;
The rich, the rabbis, such a noble throng
As Bethlehem had never seen before,
And may not see again. And here they were,

Close herded with their servants, till the inn was like a
   hive at swarming-time, and I
Was fairly crazed among them.
                              Could I know
(*Two hands spread-eagled*) that they were so important?
Just the two
—No servants; just a workman sort of man,
Leading a donkey, and his wife thereon,
Drooping and pale—I saw them not myself
(*Hand movements are important*), my servants must have
   driven them away;
But had I seen them, how was I to know?
(*shrugging shoulders*) Were inns to welcome stragglers, up
   and down
in all our towns from Beer-Sheba to Dan.
Till He should come? And how were men to know?
There was a sign, they say, a heavenly light
(*pointing upward*)
Resplendent; but I had no time for stars.
And there were songs of angels in the air
Out on the hills; but how was I to hear
Amid the thousand clamours of the Inn?
Of course, if I had known them, who they were,
And who He was that should be born that night—
For now I learn that they will make Him King,
A second David, who will ransom us
From these Philistine Romans—who but He
That feeds an army with a loaf of bread,
And if a soldier falls, He touches him
And up he leaps, uninjured?—had I known,
I would have turned the whole inn upside down,
His Honour, Marcus Lucius, and the rest,
And sent them all to stables, had I known.
(*Hand movements, as though sending someone away.*)
So you have seen Him, stranger, and perhaps
(*These lines spoken more slowly*)
Again will see Him. Prithee say for me
I did not know; and if He comes again,
As he will surely come, with retinue
And banners and an army, tell my Lord
That all my inn is His to make amends.

Alas, alas! to miss a chance like that!
This inn that might be chief among them all,
The birthplace of Messiah—had I known!
(*Stage lights dim—soft music*)

Choir: 1st verse—'In the bleak mid-winter,' or simple
recorded music. (*A simple blue cloth thrown over Inn
scene and chairs placed in position will make an interior
for Herod's palace.*)

*Scene—Few palm trees and curtain in front of manger scene.
Enter narrator (dressed as a king) and three other kings with
retinue, spotlights picking them up as they come down the aisle—
stage dimly lit.*)

Narrator:
A cold coming we had of it,
Just the worst time of the year
For a journey, and such a long journey:
The way's deep and the weather sharp,
The very dead of winter.

Caspar:
And the camels galled, sore-footed, refractory,
Lying down in the melting snow.

Melchior:
There were times we regretted
The summer palaces on slopes, the terraces,
And the silken girls bringing sherbet.

Caspar:
Then the camel men cursing and grumbling
And running away, and wanting their liquor and women,

Belthazar:
And the night-fires going out, and the lack of shelters,
And the cities hostile and the towns unfriendly
And the villages dirty and charging high prices:

Narrator:
A hard time we had of it.
At the end we preferred to travel all night,
Sleeping in snatches,
With the voices singing in our eyes, saying
That this was all folly. . .
(*Lights out. Narrator and kings exit, and Bible reader
enters, picked up by spotlight*)

Bible Reader: Jesus was born in Bethlehem, in Judea, in the days when Herod was king of the province. Not long after His birth there arrived from the east a party of astrologers making for Jerusalem and enquiring as they went:

(*Enter kings and retinue, moving slowly to appropriate background music.*)

Caspar (*To sentry on duty outside Herod's palace, on extremity of stage*): Where is the child born to be King of the Jews? For we saw his star in the east and we have come to pay homage to Him?

(*Sentry enters palace.*)

Bible Reader: When King Herod heard about this, he was deeply perturbed, as indeed were all the other people living in Jerusalem.

(*Enter Herod's court*)

So he summoned all the Jewish scribes and chief priests together and asked them:

Herod: Where is he, who is called the Christ to be born?

Priest: In Bethlehem, in Judea, for this is what the prophet wrote about the matter:

Scribe (*reading scroll*):

And thou Bethlehem, land of Judah,

Art in no wise least among the princes of Judah:

For out of thee shall come forth a governor,

Which shall be shepherd of my people Israel.

Bible Reader: Then Herod invited the wise men to meet him privately (*enter wise men, after departure of the scribes and priests*), and found out from them the exact time when the star appeared. Then he sent them off to Bethlehem, saying:

Herod: When you get there, search for this little child with the utmost care.

(*Stage in semi-darkness, only enough light to see outline of characters*)

Narrator: And now the star, which they had seen in the east, went in front of them as they travelled.

(*Enter kings and retinue*)

Melchior: Then at dawn we came down to a temperate valley, wet, below the snow line, smelling of vegetation. With a running stream and a water-mill beating the darkness.

And three trees on the low sky,
And an old white horse galloped away in the meadow.

Caspar:

Then we came to a tavern with vine leaves over the lintel,
Six hands at an open door dicing for pieces of silver,
And feet kicking the empty wine-skins.

Belthazar:

But there was no information, and so we continued,
And arrived at evening, not a moment too soon
Finding the place; it was (you may say) satisfactory.

(*Lights on stage, curtain removed revealing pageant of Holy Family, as wise men enter house—brighter lights on stage A, dim B*)

Bible Reader: So they went into the house and saw the little child with His mother Mary. And they fell on their knees and worshipped Him. They opened their treasures and presented Him with gifts—

Melchior:

Gold—For unto us a child is born, to us a son is given;
And the government shall be upon His shoulder.
And His name will be called
'Wonderful Counsellor, Mighty God, Everlasting
   Father, Prince of Peace.'
Of the increase of his government and of peace there will
   be no end, upon the throne of David, and over his
   kingdom, to establish it with justice and with righteous-
   ness from this time forth and for evermore.[1]

Balthazar: Frankincense—for he holds his priesthood permanently, because he continues for ever.[2]

Caspar:

Myrrh—For as it is written:
Surely He has borne our griefs and carried our sorrows:
Yet we esteemed Him stricken, smitten by God and
   afflicted.
But He was bruised for our iniquities; upon Him was the
   chastisement that made us whole, and with His stripes
   we are healed.[3]

Narrator:

All this was a long time ago, I remember,

[1]Isaiah 9: 6 and 7. [2]Hebrews 7: 24. [3]Isaiah 53: 4 and 5.

102

And I would do it again, but set down
This; were we led all this way for
Birth or death? There was a birth, certainly,
We had evidence and no doubt. I had seen birth and
    death,
But had thought they were different; this Birth was
    hard and bitter agony for us, like Death, our Death.
We returned to our places, these Kingdoms,
But no longer at ease here, in the old dispensation,
With an alien people clutching their gods.
I should be glad of another death.

4. Where are the stars?

A Christmas play for children by Elspeth Stephenson.

CAST

Ann	Chinese Boy
Peter	Other Children
Angel	Other Angels
Chinese Girl	Wise Men
Indian Girl	Shepherds
African Boy	Mary

SCENE 1—The Children's Bedroom

*L., back, parted screens or draped curtains to represent a long
window.*
*R., back or side—according to the depth of the stage—two
small beds which—if necessary —may be made up on forms or
chairs. At the foot of each hangs an empty stocking. The lighting,
which is dim, comes from the window, where Ann and Peter
stand listening to the choir, singing either 'God rest you Merry,
Gentlemen', or 'The First Nowell'. The children join in the
singing now and again, and Peter turns a somersault or two on
the floor, goes to look in his empty stocking, and wanders back to
the window as the carol ends.*
Ann (*after peering out of the window to see the last of the
    singers*):   There, they've all gone away now, so I suppose
    we had better get back to bed, Peter.

103

(*She gets demurely into hers, and Peter takes a flying leap at his*). O-oh, isn't it cold?

Peter (*sitting up and hugging his knees*): Rather—my teeth are chattering. I say, Ann, look at that very bright star. (*He points across at the window.*) Right up there—no silly, you're not looking in the right place—a bit farther that way.

Ann (*craning to see*): Well, I can't see round corners, you know. Oh, yes, I see it now. It is a beauty, isn't it? And it seems to grow bigger as you look at it.

Peter: I've never seen such a whopping star.

Ann: It looks to me very much like the one the carol-singers were singing about just now.

Peter: Do you mean the one that led the Wise Men to the Baby Jesus?

Ann: Yes. Oh, Peter, don't you think it must have been lovely following a star for miles and miles and then getting to Bethlehem?

Peter (*considering*): Well, it depends how far it was.

Ann: Wouldn't it be wonderful if that great star could take us to Bethlehem? (*She lies down.*)

Peter: I shouldn't mind if I could be a Wise Man and take Him a present.

Ann: You mean the Baby? Well, I should take Him a present anyway. Lie down now, Peter.

Peter (*snuggling down in bed*): What would you take Him?

Ann: The best thing I have—my umbrella.

Peter: What could a baby do with that? I should take Him my bunny gloves.

Ann (*sitting up again*): Peter, it's very late—it must be almost Christmas Day, and time for Father Christmas to come. Shall we stay awake and see him?

Peter (*yawning loudly*): Oh, yes, let's; but I'm going to shut my eyes just for a few minutes first.

Ann: You mustn't do that or you know what will happen—you'll go right off to sleep and miss everything.

Peter (*sleepily*): Well, you can wake me when he comes.

Ann: All right. I don't suppose it will be long before he's here. We ought to be able to see him splendidly; that star makes the room almost as bright as day.

Peter: Don't forget to wake me. (*Ann lies down again*).

(After a pause Ann begins singing softly the first verse of 'O come, all ye faithful!' The light from the window increases, and an ANGEL appears.)

Ann (breaking off her singing and sitting up quickly): Oh, how bright! And look, Peter, here's an angel. *(She springs out of bed and shakes her brother.)* Peter!

Peter: Leave me alone.

Ann: An angel, Peter. Do wake up quickly.

Peter (raising his head): An angel? Whatever for?

Ann: I don't know yet. *(To Angel)* Please, what have you come for?

Angel (standing with folded hands at the foot of the beds). You wanted to follow the Star to Bethlehem to find the Christ-child.

Ann: Yes, but of course we know we can't.

Angel: Why not?

Peter: It's too late.

Ann: That happened nearly two thousand years ago.

Angel: But it is never too late to find the Christ-child.

Ann: Isn't it?

Peter: How?

Angel: By following the Star.

Peter: Where?

Angel: To Bethlehem. *(He beckons them to follow and, turning, walks towards the window.)*

Ann: To Bethlehem! *(excited)* Oh, Peter!

Peter: Is this real or is it a dream? *(Angel stands waiting.)*

Ann: Hush—let us follow quietly. *(She leads Peter towards the Angel, then stops suddenly.)* Oh, please will you wait a moment? If we really are going to Bethlehem we must take our presents, Peter.

Peter: Oh, ra-ther! *(They run off, R., and return immediately with the umbrella and gloves.)* Now we are quite ready to come.

Angel (pointing off, L.): There is the Star. Follow where its clear shining shall lead you.

Ann: But aren't you coming with us?

Angel (shaking head): I must bring other children who would see the Christ-child this night, for this night of Christmas belongs to children the world over. But I shall be with you when you are come to Bethlehem.

Ann (rather breathlessly):   To Bethlehem! It sounds true, but I can't believe it is. Come, Peter.

(The CHILDREN walk slowly off, L., their eyes on the star outside. The Angel follows them. Unseen choir sings 'Angels from the Realms of Glory'.)

SCENE II—Outside the stable

The screens set L. back for Scene I remain. Another screen conceals the two beds, R. back. Yet another screen is set diagonally R. front to represent the entrance to stable, guarded by two Angels. Star hangs over stable. As the hymn ends more Angels and many Children enter, L. back, and L. and R. front. Enter Ann and Peter, followed by Angel. As Peter speaks, all the Angels withdraw.

Peter: Oh, look at all these other children, Ann.

Ann: Yes, boys and girls from different countries, too.

Peter: Different coloured skins—black and yellow and brown and white. I didn't think they knew about the Baby Jesus. Why do you think they have come?

Ann: I'll ask one of them *(To Chinese Girl)* What have you come here to see?

Chinese Girl: Why, the Christ-child, of course.

Ann (to Indian Girl):   And you?

Indian Girl: The Christ-child.

Peter: We didn't think you knew about Him.

Indian Girl: Some of us do; and, anyway, He belongs to us just as much as He belongs to you.

African Boy: He belongs to all of us.

Ann: But how did you get here?

African Boy: We followed the star.

All Children (in three-part chorus):   So did we. We all did. That's how I came.

Indian Girl: We wanted to see the Christ-child born in Bethlehem. I've brought my shell beads to give Him.

Ann: I've brought my umbrella.

Chinese Girl: I've brought my best embroidered coat.

African Boy: I've brought some arrows I made myself.

Peter: And I've brought Him my bunny gloves.

(The children, clustering in little groups, talk quietly together. The little CHINESE BOY stands apart, covering his gift with his wide sleeve.)

106

Ann (to Chinese Girl): What a lovely coat!

Indian Girl: I like your umbrella.

Chinese Girl: And your shell beads are very pretty.

Peter: I wish I had some arrows like those.

African Boy (capering round in Peter's gloves): These little pelts fit me finely.

Ann: But we can't give them to each other because we want them all for the Baby.

All Children: Yes, of course we do.

Ann (to little Chinese Boy: Why do you stand so far apart? What are you hiding.?

Chinese Boy (showing his gift): I could only bring Him my bowl of rice. When I saw all your fine presents, it seemed too poor to offer him, but it was for my meal and it's all I have. Do you think He will mind very much?

Ann (kindly): I don't think He'll mind. It's a very nice little bowl, anyway.

(Unseen choir sings the first verse of 'O come, all ye faithful'. Ann continues speaking through the singing. Listen, there's someone singing, and (looking off L.) there are heaps more people coming.

The CHILDREN group themselves, back, as the ANGELS enter in slow procession, followed by the Wise Men and Shepherds. The guardians of the stable remove the screen(s), revealing the Holy Family. WISE MEN and SHEPHERDS kneel in adoration, the CHILDREN close in behind them, standing; ANGELS surround the group, in semi-circle. One by one the WISE MEN advance and lay their gifts at MARY'S feet, pressing the edge of the Baby's shawl to their lips before returning to their places.)

Peter (in loud whisper to ANGEL): Can we take Him our presents now? *(Angel nods)* Go on, Ann, you go first.

Ann goes forward and lays her umbrella reverently beside the WISE MEN'S gifts. She kisses the edge of the shawl, and kneels. PETER follows, and then the other CHILDREN, one by one, until all have laid down their gifts and are kneeling at MARY'S feet. The last in the procession is the little CHINESE BOY. As Mary speaks, the guardian ANGELS pick up the children's gifts and hand them to her.

Mary: The Christ-child's joy is that all dear children should share their gifts in Him at Christmas-tide; so *(she beckons*

107

to ANN, who rises and comes close to her) to you He gives this
lovely coat (*ANN moves back and kneels again*) To you (*she
beckons Peter*) these arrows (*PETER kneels again:*) these
beads shall rest on your pretty neck (*CHINESE GIRL
accepts them and kneels again;*) *MARY turns to the AFRI-
CAN BOY* these furry gloves shall please your little heart
(*she beckons the little CHINESE BOY to her and takes his
hand in hers*)*;* and from your bowl of rice shall all his
hungry friends be fed, little brother. (*She kisses him on the
forehead, and he kneels again.*) And now to each of you
the Christ-child gives His own gift—the Star of Peace
and Joy—and bids you love him well.

Ann: I know we all want to say thank you, but we don't know
how to say it. So may we sing Him our song instead?
(*Mary nods her head.*)

(*Chorus of CHILDREN*): 'Away in a Manger'.

*During the singing of the first two verses each child is given
a lighted star which it holds in its right hand; at the beginning
of the last verse all lighting, except for the stars, is extinguished. At the conclusion of the carol the CHILDREN
rise, while the music continues, and after circling the stage
once, move out L. back, leaving the WISE MEN and
SHEPHERDS still kneeling. Unseen choir: 'O come,
all ye faithful' (second verse.)*

SCENE III—Same as Scene I

*Angel leads in Ann and Peter, L. back. The light shines in from
window, and the Children carry their lighted stars in their hands.*

Ann: Why, we're home again!

Peter: Is this Christmas morning?

Ann: Yes, I think so, but it's still the middle of the night.
I suppose we shall have to go to bed again and sleep till
morning. (*Turning to ANGEL*) May we truly keep the
stars?

Angel: You will lose them and you will find them, and then
they will be yours just as long as you love the Christ-
child who gave them to you.

Peter: How shall we lose them?

Ann: How shall we find them?

Angel: You will find them when you kneel as you knelt
before the Babe. (*Exit.*)

Peter: He's gone. Had you ever seen an angel before, Ann?

Ann: Don't be silly—you know I hadn't. Oh, Peter, it was wonderful, wasn't it?

Peter (*yawning*): Yes, it was, but it's made me awfully sleepy. (*They both get into bed, still holding their stars.*)

Ann: I'm sleepy too.

Peter: Hold your star tight. The angel said we should lose them, I don't mean to lose mine.

Ann (*drowsily*): What a lovely present to give us! Good night, Peter. Are you asleep yet?
(*There is no reply. In the pause that follows the star lights vanish, the daylight grows brighter, showing the sleeping CHILDREN and a well-filled stocking at the foot of each bed.*)

Peter (*sitting up suddenly*): Wake up, wake up, Ann. It's Christmas morning. Merry Christmas!

Ann (*scrambling up*): Merry Christmas! Oh, look, the stockings are full!

Peter (*excited*): Why, here are my arrows—just what I wanted.

Ann: And here is the embroidered coat—oh, it's a lovely dressing gown! Look at the colours, Peter—aren't they beautiful?

Peter: But the stars—where are the stars?
(*They search for them.*)

5. We want the truth

An idea for presentation of the Evidence for Easter to teenagers and/or adults by Patrick Goodland
A documentary presentation of some of the evidence for the death and resurrection of Jesus Christ.
The setting is a T.V. studio. Much of the reporting can be taped. Various adaptations with pictures, film and visuals could be incorporated. Suitable slides can be hired or purchased. See Appendix.
Two T.V. monitors on a panel with a few lights and switches make up the main set. These can be simply constructed out of cardboard packing cases. Back projection of slides or films can be accomplished by using strong tracing paper screens.
The Coffee Bar scene can be acted out, and is capable of

expansion with music. Waitresses could serve the audience if the performance hall is set out carefully. The keynote is informality, but careful preparation and rehearsal are imperative in this multi-media presentation.

CAST—In order of appearance:

Producer—Director.
Reporter—Paul Adelphos.
Old Woman—Salome.
Man in Street.
Young Woman—Hagar Hasmonea.
Reporter—Timothy Cassius.
Reporter—Ismael Levinson.
Pontius Pilate.
Reporter—Jacob Stein.
Sgt. Plubius.
Cpl. Jonas.
Reporter—Adrian Benhadad.
Joseph of Arimathea.
Reporter—Geoffrey Tyre.
Zaccheus.
Voice 1.
Voice 2.
Voice 3.
T.V. Secretary.

EASTER STORY

Props and Music.
Desk with screens.
Slide pictures of
Paul.
Adelphos on
screen. Pl.

Paul Adelphos:

(*Scene: News Desk, T.V. Producer sitting at desk introduces—*)
Late News from the Middle East, the cauldron of trouble, centres today on Jerusalem. For a full report of the latest developments we go over to Paul Adelphos.

Jerusalem city, scene of many battles, human tragedies and crises since its founding by King David a thousand years ago, and enlarged by his despotic son King Solomon, has erupted into crisis again today.

Early this morning rumours have startled the city and filtered into the surrounding villages of Bethany and Air Karim concerning a young revolutionary teacher called Jesus.

He was hanged outside the city wall last Friday—the charge was treason, put up by the religious leaders. The speed and fury of the trial which took place in dubious circumstances aroused quite a lot of local feeling.

Demonstrations of hate and loyalty have divided the city. This small-town artisan became a hot potato in a city which is full of pilgrims gathered for the Jewish Festival of the Passover. The streets tonight, as I look out from our studio perched on the city overlooking Gethsemane, are quiet. Pilate's police have cleared them, and a curfew has been imposed. This religious teacher certainly caused a storm in his short three-year teaching career in the towns and villages of Palestine. In hanging Jesus, the authorities were sure that they'd silenced this revolutionary—but, and it's a big but, tonight the city is buzzing with rumours. People are saying that Jesus is alive. Everyone is asking 'Is it possible for someone who suffered so much, hanging on a cross and then being sealed in a grave for three days—to come alive again! The whole episode has set this city alight with speculation, for their traditions and Scriptures lead these Jews to believe in a Messiah who would come and set them free.

Believe you me, many of them despise their Roman overlords and masters. This was demonstrated just over a week ago when the young rebel Jesus rode in on a

111

donkey to the acclaim of thousands. He looked like a victorious king that day, and there seems little doubt that he shook both the staid religious leaders and the Roman authorities. When he went to the Temple on Tuesday last, and attacked the ecclesiastical system and hotly condemned them for pulverizing the poor, the fat was really in the fire. He overturned money-changers' tables, drove out men and sacrificial sheep—there was pandemonium. Terrified animals were mixed up with cursing priests, people scrambled for bits of money—they're very attached to material things—pigeons set up a victory roll performance. The whole scene was one of confusion and chaos with the young Jesus shouting out 'This temple was made for simple prayer and worship —you have made it a den of iniquity.' The mass of people were now solidly behind him—he could have done anything that day—even clearing out the Romans, some say. But he quietly slipped out and lost his opportunity. Thursday night he was pulled in, betrayed, we are told by informed observers, by one of his closest friends.

The atmosphere is tense.

This man condemned—the verdict was signed by the Governor General, was executed on Friday he was taken down before sunset and placed in the tomb of a well-known and honoured member of Jewish parliament, Joseph of Arimathea.

This morning something happened which we are still trying to unravel. The city is agog with the rumour that Jesus is alive. It is difficult to determine at this precise moment how this has occurred—but no official denial has been made. There is no doubt that something very strange is going on. A few minutes ago Caiaphas, the High Priest, drove up to the Governor General's house. He looked tired and tense and appeared alarmed and, going up the numerous steps to the house, he tripped over his petticoat-like gown. It seems quite possible that something quite momentous has taken place.

Early today my colleague, Jeremy Silas, went out with the roving microphone into the narrow streets to get accounts from local inhabitants and visitors—here is his report.

SCENE 2

Street noises.
Talking, sheep
baaing
Salome:
(Motherly
Charac.)

(Reporter): Morning, ma'am, would you like to comment on the rumour that Jesus is alive?

He was a good man, a good man. I liked his face, sincere he was, sincere. You know that I mean—open face, you know, open face, very sincere.

Reporter: Yes, what about this idea that he's alive?

Salome: Well, you know how rumours get around in this city—very religious we are, you know, very religious. Yes, I go to church every Saturday.

Reporter: But do you think Jesus is alive?

Salome: Well, he could be, but it's a bit of a mouthful, isn't it, you know. I'm religious, but this would have to be a miracle if he's come alive again. I dun'no what to think.

Reporter: Excuse me, sir. This story about Jesus being alive today after being buried. Do you believe this?

Man: Impossible! Preposterous! Just not physically possible. When you're dead, you're dead—a load of clay, that's all—there's no hope after you're dead of coming

113

	alive. No, this is just what you mass media boys make up—sensation-mongers, that's what you are! Alive from the dead—physically impossible.
Reporter:	Madam, may I ask your name?
Hagar (a young woman)	Hagar Hasmonea.
Reporter:	What do you think of this rumour that Jesus the carpenter has risen from the dead?
Hagar:	Well, he said he would—and he seemed honest enough. I think there's something in it because I hear him preaching in our village not long ago. He was so nice and simple, you could understand what he was saying.
Reporter:	You think this is true—that he's alive somewhere now?
Hagar:	Everything that I heard him say seemed honest and true—he said something when I heard him talking to the crowds in our village about the third day when he would rise again. I've no doubt this is possible, and I'm hoping to learn more before nightfall.
Reporter:	So you are prepared to believe in . . .
Programme Director:	We have just heard that our outside camera team have secured an interview with His Highness the Governor General. We take you over now to the royal residence where Timothy Cassius will describe the scene.
Timothy C:	Here in this royal residence where successive Roman Governors have held court, all is now quiet after the bustle of recent hours. The High Priest and retinue left just over an hour ago by the back door to avoid the press and camera-men. One observer described the face of Caiaphas as the colour of the scarlet rugs which adorn this palace. No official

114

comment has been made concerning the hurried conference, but we hope in a moment or two to interview Pontius Pilate.

Jerusalem is not an enviable posting for a Roman Governor—it is considered by many political commentators to be a backwater station of office. I can now see Pilate; he is in his middle fifties, greying hair, and wearing his official insignia, moving to his seat. Over to Ismael Levinson in the court room of the royal residency.

I.L.:   Lord Pilate, thank you for granting us the privilege of an interview. Would you care to comment on the crisis concerning Jesus?

Pilate (confident and relaxed):   Well, of course, it's not a crisis, nothing really has happened to bring this to crisis pitch. We have the situation well under control. Our troops are in command and our Jewish friends are very happy. There really is no cause for alarm.

I.L.:   Thank you for that assurance—but strong rumours about Jesus are. . . .

Pilate (breaking in):   Jesus was crucified on Friday. He's dead, I signed the certificate, and he's buried—that's the end of the matter. I see no point in discussing him again.

I.L.:   But there are persistent rumours that he is alive and has been seen.

Pilate (smirking):   Alive, you say! Do you mean that you are really convinced that there is a shred of evidence to prove such a fatuous statement? Come, Mr. Levinson, you are not so quickly taken in, I'm sure.

I.L.:   But Jerusalem is abuzz with talk of Jesus being a. . . .

Pilate: Well, you know what these hot-headed Jews and Arabs are like—They put spice

	with anything—walk down David's street, it stinks with spice—runs over into their talk—This is Jerusalem, my dear boy, with all its emotions and festivities. Don't believe a word of it.
I.L.:	Can you comment then, sir, on the events at the tomb early this morning?
Pilate:	What exactly do you mean?
I.L.:	Earthquake. That great stone rolled away from the mouth of the tomb?
Pilate:	Oh, that was just the work of a few skylarkers. Vandalism is on the increase—these pranks happen often in this city.
I.L.:	But don't you think this extraordinary—guards of the Palace, I believe, were on duty?
Pilate:	Well, that was a little unfortunate, but actually they were not men of the 10th Legion, but the Jewish army—good fellows, but a little careless sometimes.
I.L.:	They didn't seem very efficient—was there panic?
Pilate:	No, no, no, no—just a little problem of miscalculation.
I.L.:	Why did you place a guard on a dead man's tomb?
Pilate:	Well—(*playing for time*) as a matter of fact the circumstances were to say the least a little difficult, but it was thought advisable by the Jewish authorities—something to do with their strange religion.
I.L.:	I thought this was a political issue, not religious? Wasn't Jesus executed for high treason against the State?
Pilate:	Why, of course, Mr. Levinson. Jesus said he was king of the Jews, and we really couldn't allow that—that must be obvious. He was a bit of an anarchist, and I can't allow that in my capacity as Governor General.

	At his fair trial I gave him a chance to get out of that one, but the damned fellow wouldn't be helped—maintained he was a king. No other course open to me but to agree with the judgment of Caiaphas.
I.L.:	But what about this religious side of the issue you mentioned?
Pilate:	Yes, he was very earnest—I thought jolly brave—and he stuck to his story and convictions. The whole thing became quite difficult, quite difficult.
I.L.:	How?
Pilate:	Why—because he said he was God: imagine that, God! All very difficult for the High Priest to stomach, you know—terribly disturbing.
I.L.:	So the guard was set because he was an extraordinary prisoner and you thought that there might be something in his claim?
Pilate:	Oh no, but the High Priest did, and we put men to death rightly every day. We're determined to have a clean respectable city—but it's not often we put 'God—ha, ha—(*P. chuckles*) to death', so we had to take some extra precautions. I suppose God could wake up and there really would be trouble then! (*P. smiles*).
I.L.:	Can you also put a guard on people's mouths and silence their witness about his resurrection?
Pilate (in cynical voice):	Well, that is a little more difficult. The impossible can be done today! The miracle must take a little longer.
I.L.:	You must be a good assessor of men. What did you really think about Jesus?
Pilate:	Good fellow, exhibitionist, gift of gab, strong, healthy blighter—quite a leader, but a schizoid—difficult chap to tame.
I.L.:	Was he mad?

Pilate:	No—but strange—seemed miles away at times, but very concerned about people.
I.L.:	Was he afraid?
Pilate:	No—seemed a bit of a fatalist—thought the plan of life was going as it should, I suppose. He wasn't afraid of me—you would have thought I was being judged the way he behaved. It didn't worry him that with one flick of my little finger I could make him a dead man. In the end I had no option open. I tried to help him—he wouldn't be helped. I had to condemn him.
I.L.:	But you weren't sure he was really good material for slaughter?
Pilate:	He was young, intelligent, as I said, a bit of a leader—but on the wrong side. We can't have revolutionaries.
I.L.:	So you condemned him?
Pilate:	I had to—there might have been serious repercussions—a riot or some religious rift. I had to agree to his execution.
I.L.:	Out of duty then?
Pilate:	Well, if you like to put it that way.
I.L.:	You feel that's the end of the episode?
Pilate:	Yes I do.
I.L.:	But this strange rumour persists. Do you really think it's the end?
Pilate:	Well I (ah) . . . I'm a . . . Yes, I do.
I.L.:	Thank you, Lord Pilate.

SCENE 3

Producer:	While the Governor General has been giving his interview, new developments have been taking place in the gaudy palace of Lord Caiaphas—High Priest. He holds the highest office in the Jewish religious set-up. We understand that the Sanhedrin—members of high cabinet rank—have been hastily called together. These men are powerful administrators

118

controlling the social, as well as religious, scene in Palestine.

From reports now coming on to my desk it is obvious that Sanhedrin members were not expecting to be called out tonight. One commented, as he entered the impressive palace, that he was 'fed up to the teeth with this Jesus business.' He went on to say that this was bound to affect the nation's morals. The bombastic young people would follow these revolutionary trends—he had no idea where it would end. 'Next thing,' he said, 'we shall be hearing that women are as important as men in our society! They'll be shouting about their rights.' We suspect that, like most other men in the cabinet, he is a hard-line conservative. The well-known and much-respected Mr. Nicodemus, the eminent lawyer, is quoted as saying that this case has been badly mishandled. He is known to have been sympathetic to Jesus, and made himself personally responsible for the burial.

Street Noise

There is no hope of getting into the palace as the temple guard in their colourful uniforms are at every entrance and window.

Marching feet

The military are patrolling the narrow streets and it is noticeable that groups of people are not being allowed to congregate on the streets. There is an air of tension and one topic of conversation. The obvious question that is being asked here this evening is 'Where is the body, if it's still a corpse?' Some are openly saying that the hierarchy could stop all the rumours and blow the lid off this tense situation by simply putting the body on show. Maybe this is what the Sanhedrin are planning to do at the moment.

119

Jacob Stein of Jerusalem T.V. is now actually in the city wall Coffee Bar. He is hoping to interview some witnesses of events which have taken place in Jerusalem in the last 72 hours. We go over now to the Coffee Bar.

Jacob S.: The rather depressing atmosphere of the quiet Jewish Sabbath is over. But as the crowds walked up the steps to the Lion Gate in the old city there was incessant talk about the empty tomb. The question—did Jesus rise from the dead?—is on everyone's lips. Much embarrassment is felt in the city.

Music in background. General hum of conversation. Here in this snug coffee bar atmosphere, a happy hunting ground for the troops seeking light relief, there are many young people, students and soldiers, their gaiety and fun, their dancing and laughter contrasting sharply with the bearded, dignified solemnity of the elders in the streets outside.

We had difficulty in getting our cameras in tonight, even the brash military are a bit edgy—there is this air of uncertainty. I would like to introduce to you Sgt. Plubius of the 10th Legion.

You've been stationed in Jerusalem nearly two years?

Plubius: Yeah, that's right. Two years come May.

Jacob S.: Your home is in Rome?

Plubius: Yeah, now that's a place for life, plenty of sports, lion fights, boozers and delicious women! . . .

Jacob S.: Quite so, quite so. But Sgt., how have you found this tour in Palestine?

Plubius: Do you jolly well want to know? HOT, arid and generally unfriendly. These religious fanatics are always causing trouble. Now I've nothing against religion myself—I pray to my gods when I'm in

	a tight corner, but this lot, they're always squabbling about trifles—the blackguards, they say one thing and do another. Can't trust 'em.
Jacob S.:	You must have had some hectic moments recently by all accounts?
Plubius:	Yeah! I was on detachment on the Calvary job last Thursday. I've done a number of these in my time, but this one was different.
Jacob S.:	This was the afternoon when Jesus and the two thieves were hung up?
Plubius:	Yeah—it was pretty dreadful, so many weeping women who wouldn't go away. The old flaming, flat-footed High Priest was really worked up—you should have seen his small fry whipping up the crowd into a frenzy—I thought their heads would roll off with all the wagging, shouting and screaming for murder they turned on. It was hellish.
Jacob S.:	It really was a bit of a stir up then?
Plubius:	I'll say—my boys had mocked this Jesus fellow and whipped him before the march—he was weak as we marched him along the route, but there was something different about him. He didn't curse and swear like others.
Jacob S.:	You mean he was like a gentleman even when tortured and facing death?
Plubius:	I've never experienced anything like it. Kind of calmness and acceptance. I could have belted those priestly fellows, especially those young 'uns. I bet they would have yelped the moment we laid a hand on them—but Jesus now . . .
Jacob S.:	He was brave and different then. How about the crunch when the nails were driven in?
Plubius:	Most extraordinary. He still didn't curse and struggle—he was like a lamb. When

121

	we yanked the cross up and slammed it down in the hole, his body weight tore the flesh of his hands, but he still didn't curse us. He was so different.
Jacob S.:	This really is beginning to tie up with the other things we have heard.
Plubius:	But what really struck me was later, when my boys had as usual gambled for his rather nice tweedy coat, and the clouds began to wrap around us, and it became dark—he wouldn't take the grog to help him which I put on a sponge on the end of my spear. But you know he thanked me, he thanked me—I can't forget it— he thanked me—and I'd been part of the crew who'd tortured him. But most strange of all was his dying whispers—he said 'Father, Father, forgive these fellows here, they don't know what they've done'.
Jacob S.:	This is strange—what do you make of it?
Plubius:	Well, he said he was God—he sure acted like one—he certainly was the bravest, finest youngster I've ever seen, that's a fact. Somehow I feel better for meeting him. It makes—you think, you know, it makes you think.
	(*dreamily*) Forgiveness, forgiveness—well by God! We all need it—if he is God, he can forgive. . . .
Jacob S. (*quickly coming in*):	You've heard the rumours going around today?
Plubius:	About the empty tomb?
Jacob S.:	Yes, they say he's risen, do you believe that?
Plubius:	Well, if anyone deserves to he does—such a fine fellow. Old Jonas of the Palace guard was there this morning on duty. He's quite jiggered tonight—muddled—I think he's trying to drink away his troubles. Hi, Jonas, come over here, I want a word with you. Tell this Mr. Jac. . . .

Jacob S.:	Jacob Stein of Jerusalem T.V.
Plubius:	What you were telling me about the tomb in Joseph's garden.
Jonas (a little bit drunk):	Is this being broadcast live—I've got me dentures out, wait a jiff. (*pops teeth in*)
Jacob S.:	Did you hear or see anything strange this morning, Corporal Jonas?
Jonas:	Didn't I just. There was a ugh! thundering great clap at about 5 a.m. just as it was getting light—'Great fire balls,' I shouted, 'What in God's name is happening'—(*gulps*) next thing there was an almighty clap of thunder, and I think a whirlwind—a blazing whirlwind (*burps*)—next thing we knew we were getting up from the ground, cursing this weather. God, my head!
Jacob S.:	What happened next?
Jomas:	Blimey, mate, was we dazed! We looked over at the tomb in the side of the wall. We nearly had kittens on the spot. (*burps*)
Jacob S.:	Yes, go on—
Jonas:	That blinking great stone which took four of us to roll into place (*burp*) had rolled over, the grave was open and bloomin' well empty, just clothes—like an Egyptian mummy. The myrrh and aloes holding 'em together like. Cor, it was uncanny.
Jacob S.:	What was your next move?
Jonas:	We went to the priest. Were they furious! Blimey mate, their looks nearly put me in the tomb. They had a quick shifty with the High Priest and . . .
Jacob S.:	What happened next?
Jonas:	Then they took us in and gave us a real do of a breakfast. You would have thought we were the Governor himself.
Jacob S.:	Did they talk about the empty tomb?
Jonas:	Well they did among themselves, and after breakfast one of them long-skirted

123

fellows got up and in a very monotonous tone congratulated us for the 'splendid job we'd done,' said something about a medal, then he gave us a handful of cash—I think this was a bribe to keep us quiet—well, doesn't matter where it comes from, I'm always happy to earn an honest penny.

Jacob S.: But what about the empty tomb with no body?

Jonas: Oh, they said we were to tell anyone who asked, that his friends came and stole him away.

Jacob S.: Did they?

Jonas: What them! No, they had bolted into some funk hole. Do you think they would have had a chance with us—not on your life, mate! Imagine how the other boys in the barracks would laugh at us— 'Fishermen beat up royal guards.'
Not on your nellie.

Jacob S.: So you think he did rise again?

Jonas: You asking me a straight question?

Jacob S.: Yes, did he rise again?

Jonas: Either that, or I'm going mad. He must have done! He must have done! How about another drink?

Producer: (Switch back to studio) Because of its intriguing nature, this late evening broadcast is being prolonged— other scheduled programmes have been cancelled. We have heard that the Sanhedrin has now broken up. Adrian Benhadad is waiting in the garden of the home of Joseph who lives in Arimathea. Are you there, Adrian? Come in—

Adrian B.: Yes, I'm here. I am standing in the scented garden of a large house belonging to Joseph. Even at night this place has a cool and distinctive beauty of its own. Candles flicker in the windows of the house, lighting up the neatly edged flower beds. I hear footsteps—I hope to have a word with Mr. Joseph. He is the nicest of fellows and one of the few men of independent thought and liberal view on the Sanhedrin.

Good evening, sir—I'm sorry to surprise you and to trouble you so late in the evening. Would you care to comment on this evening's meeting of the cabinet?

Joseph: This is rather high-handed, isn't it, way-laying me in my own garden?

Adrian B.: The fact is, sir, the world is wanting to know more about this Jesus fellow.

Joseph (*thoughtfully*): Yes, I can understand that.

Adrian B.: Could you tell us—is an official statement to be made about the rumour that Jesus has risen from the dead this morning?

Joseph: No official communication will be issued.

Adrian B.: But you have been discussing this subject tonight in the special cabinet meeting.

Joseph: You could say that.

Adrian B.: I believe you had some mild sympathies with Jesus?

Joseph: You could imply that, I suppose.

Adrian B.: Do you think he was a crook, or a man born before his time, a wag or a fool. . . .

Joseph: I don't think you ever met the man.

Adrian B.: But they say he's alive. He walked out of the grave in your garden this morning. Is that right?

Joseph: Only God could do a thing like that.

Adrian B.: Precisely—and that's who he said he was, didn't he?

Joseph: Yes! but that is inconceivable according to our religion.

Adrian B.: Is the High Priest worried by the empty tomb?

Joseph: He may be.

Adrian B.: Are you going to exhibit the body?

Joseph: We have no plans at the moment to do so.

125

Adrian B.:	Is this because you don't have the body in your possession?
Joseph:	(*Pause*) Well . . . em, that is a question that I am not at liberty to discuss.
Adrian B.:	But lots of people have seen the empty grave today. Wouldn't it stop rumours if you showed the body?
Joseph:	Yes, it probably would.
Adrian B.:	Sir, may I be so bold as to ask a direct question. Do you think Jesus is alive?
Joseph:	Alive? That's nigh impossible.
Adrian B.:	But you are quoted as saying at the trial that the cabinet may be fighting greater forces—even God—if they put Jesus to death. Is that statement correct?
Joseph (*thoughtfully*):	Yes, empty, empty.
Adrian B.:	Perhaps he is God's Son and you've all made a great mistake.
Joseph:	I hope not.
Adrian B.:	But you're not sure—Jesus could be alive now?
Joseph:	Yes—he could be. Goodnight, I'm tired, it's been a long day.

SCENE 4

	(This section owes a great deal to *The Davidson Affair* by Stuart Jackman.)
Producer Link Man:	While we have been on the air, news has been coming in from our man in Jericho. He has ferreted out a zealous follower of Jesus. Here is his recorded report:
Geoffrey Tyre:	Geoffrey Tyre reporting. A few minutes ago I returned from the house of a notorious tax-man in Jericho. When I arrived this afternoon, furniture and carpets of considerable value were being taken out of the front door to waiting vans. I found Zaccheus directing operations, standing on the stairway of this prosperous, well-built house.
G.T.:	Mr. Zaccheus?

Zaccheus:	Come in, my dear boy—you've come for the bedding?
Voice:	Hey guv, where is this carpet table and chairs to go?
Zach.:	To the TEAR Fund office for their refugee funds. Now my boy—everything's going—owner on the move. Yes (directing someone else), all those eats and soups are for the children's home.
G.T.:	I think you ought to know . . .
Zach.:	That's all right, you're welcome, sorry I'm so busy.
G.T.:	But we are from. . . .
Zach.:	That's all right, I can see by your clothes you're from the destitute men's club— what would you like?
Voice 2:	How about these drapes, guv?
Zach.:	You can have them, my dear man, with my love.
G.T.:	Can I talk to you, Mr. Zaccheus?
Zach.:	Talk, yes, sure thing—what about—wait till I get my cheque book.
G.T.:	No, I don't want your money, just your comments—I'm from Jerusalem T.V.
Zach.:	From Jerusalem T.V.? What's the score then—what do you want to know?
Voice 3:	'ow about this pottery, guv?
Zach:	Oh, take it to Number 53. I diddled that old girl some years ago out of 1,000 pence—that should amply repay my debt —give her my best wishes.
G.T.:	About this Jesus fellow.
Zach:	Let's sit out in the sun lounge—it's quieter there—like a glass of vintage 65 BC?
G.T.:	I'm told you were a friend of Jesus.
Zach:	He's my best friend.
G.T.:	Was, you mean.
Zach:	No, is.
G.T.:	Do you still really believe in him?
Zach:	Believe, why of course—yes, my boy, I'm his for ever.

G.T.:	Why—I mean how can you possibly believe hin im?
Zach:	Look, old boy—when someone does what no other can do, gives you life, freedom and peace after existing without purpose in darkness and despair, you believe all right—man, it's amazing.
G.T.:	What do you mean?
Zach:	Look, my boy,—everyone knows Zaccheus in Jericho. I was a twister, knew all the fiddles, robbed the poor, a real crook without any real values. I was a real cocky—couldn't care a damn, thoroughgoing crook. Everyone knew it—so I didn't have a friend.
G.T.:	You mean here in Jericho?
Zach:	No, anywhere—they hated my guts. Then one day he came to Jericho—I hid in a tree. I'd heard so much about this chap I was afraid he would slaughter me with his tongue if he got close enough, so I hid in a tree. I'm only a pint size, as you can see.
G.T.:	Yes! Yes! go on.
Zach:	He walked down the street, stopped right under the tree and called my name. The most civil thing anyone had done for years. Then he invited himself to my house for dinner. Did the people talk—cor, they didn't half wag their tongues—Jesus, teacher, healer, good man, gone to Zach's place for nosh—'im who's been fleecing us for years, and I had—I'd milked them all right. I had a job to walk home with him—but I got Jonesy my housekeeper to lay on the best meal we'd had for years. She nearly fainted on the spot when I gave her a wadge of notes to go and buy from the market. I'd kept her tight for years. I was a mean rat.
G.T.:	You say you were, or are?

128

Zach:	Oh, no. Everything has changed since I met Jesus. He showed me what a fool I was simply trusting in money. My boy, he taught me the joy of giving. Jesus knew poverty as I did when I was a boy. Religion's an expensive thing, and neither of us could pay for birds and animals that these crooked priests sell in the temple.
G.T.:	We heard Jesus caused a rumpus last week in turning over the temple money-changers' desks.
Zach:	I'd love to have been there that day. Just imagine all that lolly rolling about—quite a party. But that's Jesus! He made God real—disrobed him and sorted him out from all the trimmings of religion. God's not locked up in church buildings, my boy; he comes into life. Jesus forgave me, and gave me his strength. Things are very different now—the Kingdom of God, he said, is in you. Can't earn it or buy it.
G.T.:	So that's why you're so generous in giving away all these things today?
Zach:	Well, yes, but Jesus gave me the priceless gift of love—I don't mean the sentimental slush which is mostly animal lust. This love seeks the best for others—opening up our minds to others—being honest and sincere even with those with whom we may disagree. That's the love we need, dear boy. Nothing can buy that, but Jesus can give it. You can't play with it—it's all or nothing. But boy, oh boy, get in that groove and you're away—you're free. You really live.
G.T.:	Where's all this freedom and love going to lead you?
Zach:	I'm going to live—LIVE!
G.T.:	But your giving up this house?
Zach:	Yes, that's right—giving it all away. I've no more use for it now.

G.T.:	That's a bit rash, isn't it?
Zach:	No, not now—you see I've no need because I've changed. I only want simple things now—really to enjoy God's wonderful world. These things are to do with my past.
G.T.:	Jesus has done this for you? I can't really begin to see how but you're very convincing.
Zach:	I'm off to meet Jesus and then we'll see about the future—but I'm sure we'll have to be busy telling others about the way.
G.T.:	You mean you really think he's alive? You're going to see him?
Zach:	Yes, absolutely sure.
G.T.:	Where?
Zach:	Not sure of the place.
G.T.:	You seem so sure he's alive. What evidence have you got?
Zach:	Mary, the converted belly dancer, told me on the 'phone this morning of her meeting with the master at about 5 a.m., in the garden—she and other women went to embalm the body, but found the grave empty.
	Pretty alarming by all accounts. But then Jesus met her—she's sure all right. No one else has the same inflection in his voice—she's just bubbling over with joy. Beautiful girl, our Mary.
	Then just an hour ago I heard that another disciple, Cleopas, has had a walk and a long talk with him today.
G.T.:	A walk and a talk—you're joking.
Zach:	No, I'm not—if you want to check this story, ring up Jer 264641, or go and call at 54a Straight Street, top floor.
G.T.:	Perhaps Cleopas, was just day-dreaming— just hoping that Jesus would come back.
Zach:	Well, you might have said that if he was just sitting still alone sunbathing, but he

was walking with his wife, and she's down to earth—calls a spade a spade all right, she does. Anyway, they were going this afternoon rather late to Emmaus, their home. With others they thought that our Master was dead and buried and that was the end of a wonderful friendship and adventure. They said they were feeling sorry for themselves, when a stranger joined, and asked if he could walk with them. He turned out to be a great teacher and explained all the Old Testament scriptures which anticipated our Master coming. He showed them that he had to die, to share every experience of man. You conquer sin and death not by avoiding it, but by challenging, accepting and breaking through it. Isn't that right, Mr. Tyre? They said they'd never heard the like. Masterly. When they got home and their guest was about to give thanks for the food, his voice sounded familiar, and then they saw his hands and the nail prints in his hands—they realized then it was Jesus.

They rushed back to Jerusalem. They haven't got any transport—it was dark and it's not safe to walk in the streets at night, but they lost all sense of fear and are now back in Jerusalem. I tell you, there's a right party going on there. Singing, praising God—such happiness—the disciples are cock-a-hoop.

(*Heavy banging upstairs*)	
G.T.:	This really is extraordinary, I must try and meet Mary—she sounds a fabulous creature.
Zach:	Excuse me, that must be my gold-plated bath being taken out—I don't want it scratched. It's going to the Home for

131

Gentlewomen in Restricted Circumstances!

Remind me to tell you about the Master's appearance to his eleven closest friends earlier today.

G.T.: This is Geoffrey Tyre—news at ten—returning you to the studio.

SCENE 5

Producer: This has been a most intriguing documentary. Changed lives—new values—hope for the world of men. Promises of a new day dawning— this is what we need.

Can this Jesus meet these demands? We leave you to sift the evidence. The last word has not been given on this extraordinary claim that Jesus has risen from the dead. We shall await developments.

As we close down tonight, I regret to announce that Rabbi Saul has refused to conduct the epilogue this evening in protest to what he calls the leftish bias and blasphemy of this documentary. His theme was to have been 'The Implications of Unbelief.'

Paper handed to PRODUCER: Late news flash. Jesus has been seen again. . . .

Telephone rings: (lifts receiver) Excuse me one moment.

(Chanting rabble heard outside.) Stop the broadcast?

Noise gradually increases. No, I certainly can't. What—The Prime Minister's instructions?

Who does he think!

'Nonsense' we want truth. What!

Shouts—set it alight. Pull it down! But this is one of the most dynamic scoops we've ever handled.

Protest—who—the High Priest?

Let 'em go to . . .

What, they're at the door?

You call this a religious state!

Intelligent democracy!

Anarchists—fear—truth—they're crazy.

Rabble rushes in up gangways, rough handles the producer—smoke bomb—red glow. Two billposters with brushes in hands unroll poster message in large letters announcing:

'This station is off the air until further notice, due to irresponsible broadcasting.'

6. I believe in protons

A play suitable for Easter and other occasions. It could be followed by group discussion.

CAST

First Student	Inventor
Second Student	Peter
Third Student	Speaker
Fourth Student	Woman of Samaria
Thinker	Narrator
Voice	Announcer
Other Students	Centurion

(*Curtain opens on student meeting*)

1st Student: And so we will recommend increased hours of service in the university refectory. Any other matters?

2nd Student: I feel we should organize a protest. After all, every other university has done so—why not us?

(*Chorus of assent*)

1st Student: Actually I'd not thought of that—but surely there's something—hasn't the Vice-Chancellor got secret files we can raid or should we have more representation on the Senate. . . .

3rd Student: Not in this place—everything's too much above-board. I agree we must have a protest—why not lots of them, but what about?

1st Student: We will think about it and find some matter to make ourselves felt.

(*End of meeting. All students make their exits. Enter Thinker.*)

Thinker: Rather a waste of time, these N.U.S. meetings—who cares if refectories open longer or squash courts cleaned more often, and even trying to organize a protest without a reason. Protest, protest . . . what is a protest but something about which one is dissatisfied. I suppose

133

basically they are all dissatisfied with themselves. Certainly that would be the psychological answer, but no one protests against himself—no one has ever protested against mankind itself. . . .

Voice: You are wrong, my friend. I have protested against mankind and yet you have not heard my protest!

Thinker: Who are you, what do you do, why do you protest?

Voice: I am a maker of things and people. I made you. But all my mankind has turned against me. Mankind knows not its Maker.

Thinker: But nobody ever heard of you—unless, of course, you are God—the one they talk about in churches, I believe. But didn't you just make this world, wind it up and let it run? Surely you're not interested in it now?

Voice: My creation is always my interest and as I see dishonesty, cowardice and darkness in my world, I grieve over it all.

Thinker: Well, you have made me think, but I must ask some more questions. (*Enter Students*) Oh, it's them again, I'd better go and join them.

(*Students with banners, etc., up to door No. 10. Shouting, knock on door. Move to other side of stage—simple door marked number 10 is sufficient scenery.*)

Freedom Song:

Hey there, Mr. Blackman, can you hear me?
I don't want your diamonds or your care
I just want to be someone known to you as me
And I will bet my life you want the same.
700 million are neglected
Most of what you read is lies
Speaking one to one, making everybody's sun
To wake me in the morning when we rise.
No doubt some folks enjoy doing battle
Like presidents, prime ministers and kings,
So let us build them shelves
So they may fight among themselves
And we must be the ones to sing.
Come and sing a simple song of freedom
Sing it like you've never done before
Let it fill the air, tell the people everywhere
That we, the people here, don't want the war.

Thinker: War, violence, men are always rough, never can we rid ourselves of man's inhumanity to man. It's useless to protest against war, really. . . .

Voice: But I have made my protest against violence in your world.

Thinker: Oh, you . . . I had forgotten you . . . Yes, now, tell me one single thing. Have you actually made any differences to this world? What changes have you made? The jungles are still red in tooth and claw, man lives ultimately only for himself, society is only an uneasy treaty between those who would destroy their neighbours if there were no repercussions. Well, what have you done for this world?

Voice: I have entered your world, like a man, in one of the most violent times in history. I came to peasants and was born as their child, I walked the dusty roads of Palestine and even. . . .

Thinker: You mean Jesus Christ then? Yes, I know something of that myth. True, I left Sunday School at six years old but that was enough to convince me that we can never discover who Jesus was. It's all lost in history. We have not the slightest idea what he did if he ever existed. Didn't someone write, 'The Quest of Historical Jesus'—well, I bet he never found him. You would need a time-machine for that.

Voice: All right, you need a time-machine—send for the inventor.

Thinker: Send for the inventor? Who's he? (*Enter Inventor*) Who are you?

Inventor: I am an inventor. Did not someone call? What can I do for you sir?

Thinker: No, I didn't call for you . . . unless you can produce a time machine?

Inventor: Time-machine, sir, why indeed. I designed one many years back for a client who wanted to write about it. Brilliant writer he was, too, but strange thing was he only used it to look to the future. He never went into the past.

Thinker: You mean that you could make such a device again?

Inventor: In fact, I still have the prototype which I made years ago. My client had a copy of it. I'll lend it to you if you'll go into the past with it.

Thinker: Yes, yes, it's the past that interests me.

Inventor: Well, give me a hand, sir; it's just here. By the way, there is one problem. In the prototype I could not prevent a change in the third dimension as well as the fourth. This means that you will move to a new place as well as a new time. Now, if you go back into the past you will also move roughly east, probably about one and a half miles for each year you travel. It's due to the ethereal rotation of the space-time co-ordinate system. Anyway, the best of luck, sir. This is the time control, it's all very simple really.

Thinker: Seems a most strange device to me. But on your assurance I'll have a go.

Inventor: Before you go, sir . . . are you an atheist, too? The last chap who asked for one of these, Mr. Wells, was . . . but what he saw in the future made him very uneasy.

Thinker: I wouldn't call myself an atheist. Let's say an agnostic. Not made up my mind, but will need a lot of proof when I do. But thanks, I will press your lever.

(*Time travel, music, lighting, background of lake*)

Thinker: I find myself beside a lake. Is this Cumberland? No, perhaps North Italy, indeed I have no idea where I am.

(*Enter Peter*)

Thinker: My good man . . . I know not where or when I am. Tell me the name of this lake and whether the Queen be on the throne?

Peter: Do not you know that this is the Lake of Gennesaret often called Galilee? As for a Queen, there are few, unless you mean Queen Herodias, the murderess. Tiberias, the Emperor, rules us all, and mighty hardly too, from the 'Imperial City'.

Thinker: Then I am in the days of the Roman Empire. That's when that Jesus Christ was supposed to live, I think.

Peter: Ah, that name . . . it's known to you. It was but a few years back that he stood beside this lake.

Thinker: What was he like? Who was he?

Peter:

I asked that—until one day upon the dusty
road, the answer came to 'Who was he?'
We were walking despondently towards the city
Discouraged and alone. Driven from Galilee,
Each had his own regrets. Yes, even he
Was sorrowful—I, Peter, sensed it—saying little,
Scarcely answering . . . Then all at once
The sound of water. We raised our heads,
And, rearing over us, a cliff of limestone,
Brilliant in sunlight. Streaks of iron, like blood,
Ran down it, and from a cave
Half down the rock, the Jordan river
Descending from the heights of Hermon
Poured out its spring-clear waters. We stopped,
Seeing the city of Caesarea
Behind a lace of spray—the trees,
White roofs and towers. It should have lifted us,
That sudden vision. Somehow it didn't.
It made us more despondent. For I thought—
Or was it he who thought and I who felt him?
This water that is born so hopefully
Ends in the Dead Sea's useless desolation.
Abruptly he asked, 'Who do men say I am?'
We answered variously, 'John the Baptist, risen,'
'Elijah or Jeremiah,' 'One of the prophets'.
Silence, the water speaking, Then he asked:
'Who do YOU say I am?' Another silence—
Only a moment, but enough to tell
Our disillusionment. I cried—
No, rather I heard the words drawn from me—
The voice was not my own: 'You are the Christ,
Son of the living God!' He turned to me
Transfigured. His face was God's.
(*Time travel to present*)

Thinker: So that was why he came, if he ever existed—to
live among men in the violence of human life. God
among men . . . amazing!
(*Enter students in working clothes, soap box*)

1st Student: Now you workers, we have good news for you.
You have rights. Stand on your rights. Don't let the

137

bosses pull fast ones on you. You are entitled to equality. Why should they live in luxury, when you do all the work!

2nd student: Changes in society are due chiefly to the development of the internal contradictions in society, that is, the contradiction between the productive forces and the relations of production, the contradiction between classes and the contradiction between the old and the new: it is the development of these contradictions that pushes society forward and gives the impetus for the supersession of the old society by the new.

The ruthless economic exploitation and political oppression of the peasants by the landlord class forced them into numerous uprisings against its rule. . . . It was the class struggles of the peasants, the peasant uprisings and peasant wars that constituted the real motive force of historical development.

(*Song*) (*Exit student*)

Thinker: Equality, what's that? Of course all men are equal but some are more equal than others. Man is nothing but a cog in the machine of society. He has no meaning as an individual.

Voice: You poor creature, to think so lowly of yourself and of your fellow-men. I made you as individuals, with a purpose and a meaning.

Thinker: A purpose? Where is that today? Listen if you will to a thousand voices from this world who cry out that life has lost its meaning. They are the voices of the hollow men.

Speaker: We are the hollow men
We are the stuffed men
Leaning together
Headpiece filled with straw. Alas!
Our dried voices, when
We whisper together
Are quiet and meaningless
As wind in dry grass
Or rats' feet over broken glass
In our dry cellar
Shape without form, shade without colour,
Paralysed force, gesture without motion:

This is the dead land
This is cactus land
Here the stone images
Are raised, here they receive
The supplication of a dead man's hand
Under the twinkle of a fading star.
Between the desire
And the spasm
Between the potency
And the existence
Between the essence
And the descent
Falls the shadow
This is the way the world ends
Not with a bang but a whisper.

(*From 'The Waste Land' by T. S. Eliot*)

Thinker: You see, man sees no purpose in his life. What purpose did you give him when you came into his world?

Voice: An eloquent commentary upon man without his Maker. Now you listen if you will to a voice, yet one of many, that found meaning in life when I entered your world. Turn again that lever which turns the years and hear a voice from distant days.

(*Time travel—scene from Samaria; a coloured slide projected would provide adequate background*)

Thinker: Phew, this is hot indeed. Ah, yes, I can guess where I am now. This area I studied as a geography project once. It is the valley of the River Jordan leading down to the lowest point on earth, 1300 feet below sea level. And what is this village . . . There is a sign . . . Sychar . . . while just here a well—very necessary in this dry land. (*Sits on well.*)

(*Enter woman*)

Woman: Excuse me, sir. May I draw from the well?

Thinker (*getting up*): Indeed, madam . . . tell me, is this the only well for the area?

Woman: There are no others for several miles and my village on the hillside yonder has no supply. I have come here every day for years. My friends are coming, too, today, but for many long years I came alone.

Thinker: Why was that?

139

Woman: I was despised by all in my village—a crumpled
piece of humanity, until one day I met him here . . .
Jesus Christ, that is.

Thinker: Oh, him again—but tell me more.

Woman:

He came to me with his eyes and asked for water,
Stretched out his hands and spoke.
His mind turned into mine like the noon sun,
My pitcher of thoughts broke.

I had not noticed him at rest, by the well head,
Shadowed by the rare tree;
But as I carried my shame into its rare coolness,
His eyes awaited me.

I tried to avoid them as I drew the well rope,
Taut through a mindless hand,
I saw his robe cross the speckled sunlight,
His feet stir the hot sand.

I saw his face. It was white with road dust,
Whiter than any stone.
But his eyes were ageless and deep as well shafts,
As they met mine now.

They unroofed my brain with their profound gazing,
Made the heart a molten thing;
Every purdahed thought unveiled itself,
Under their questioning.

He spoke of water to cleanse the spirit;
I tried not to understand.
He followed me along the road of my evasions,
And when it ceased in sand

He brought me home from my self-forced journey—
Showed me my own soul
Cracked and dry as a discarded wine skin,
And made it whole . . .

He came to me with his eyes and asked for water,
Stretched out his hands and spoke.
As I carried my peace back to the streets of Sychar,

A new world awoke.

(*Time travel to present.*)

Thinker: So you brought hope to a desolate woman, and to many others, I daresay. But honestly, although I am impressed with this story how can I know it's true—I need proof—I cannot seek blindly.

(*Curtain opens on student group*)

2nd Student: Now what else can we protest about. We've tried war, we've tried inequality . . .

3rd Student: They only seem to be surface problems. Where is the really deep root of all our wrongs.

1st Student: Is it ignorance, perhaps?

3rd Student: Ignorance! Why of course. It's certainly true that the under-developed parts of the world are also the least educated. Wouldn't education solve all our difficulties?

2nd Student: Surely we need everyone to know the basic information about the universe. What is the most basic thing existent?

4th Student: The most fundamental thing discovered is the proton.

3rd Student: Proton? Never heard of it. Unless it's a thing in food.

4th Student: Oh, no. The proton is the smallest article that has ever been discovered within the atom structure of matter.

3rd Student: Well, then, let's make everyone believe in the existence of the proton. That would be a start at least.

2nd Student: If it's so small how can we convince anyone that it exists. After all, not many people are going to believe in a thing that they can't see, or hear, or touch, especially if the majority of the population don't believe in it.

4th Student: Wait a minute. It's not as if the proton is a figment of some scientist's imagination. There is real evidence for its existence and without it our whole picture of the atomic structure of matter would be suspect. At least I believe in protons.

3rd Student: Come on. Let's tell the world about the proton. Hyde Park is the best place to start.

(*Students march to stand with umbrellas*)

4th Student: Ladies and gentlemen, we are here this fine Sunday afternoon to reveal to you the great mystery of the proton. For an atom to be in stable equilibrium it is necessary for the positive electrical charge on the nucleus to equal the magnitude of the total charge of the electrons whose orbital positions determine the location on the periodic table. Within the nucleus are positive particles known as protons which. . . .

1st Student: Come on—nobody's listening anyway. It's not worth it.

(*Exit students*)

Thinker: Really, how naïve can you get? What a ridiculous idea to convince the world of the existence of protons. Ordinary people just don't care enough to face the facts, and why should they? Protons are only of academic interest—like gods. By the way, are you still there?

Voice: Indeed I am, and have watched with interest your reaction to these students. And you are right, ordinary people just do not care enough to face the facts, and you are among that class.

Thinker: Face the facts. That's what I am looking for. But honestly, God, my problem is to know whether you exist, whether all this you have told me is true. I can prove a proton in a laboratory, but can I prove you?

Voice: Look again then at Jesus Christ, for there you see my greatest act of communication to humanity.

Thinker: There's my difficulty. I understand that we have stories about this man, and, if true, they would be the basis of a completely new way of thinking and acting. But nobody knows whether Jesus Christ ever lived or what he did.

Curator: Excuse me interrupting, I was just passing. My name is Throgmorton; I am an assistant curator of the British Museum. Did I hear someone say that nobody knows whether Jesus Christ ever lived?

Thinker: Well, yes, I'm afraid that I said it.

Curator: Now, young man, you really should not make such stupid statements in public places.

Thinker: You mean you believe Jesus Christ lived?

Curator: Believe! I cannot doubt it. In the vaults of our Museum we have a manuscript of the Bible written within 300 years of Christ's life. In Rome is the Codex Vaticanus produced before A.D. 400. You can check these ages by the radio-active carbon test, while in Manchester are two fragments of part of the New Testament whose ink was dry before a century had elapsed from Christ's death.

Thinker: That is amazing evidence—I must try reading the Bible again. And did any of the other writers of those days mention Jesus?

Curator: Most certainly they did. Although few recognized in antiquity the impact Jesus Christ would have on the world of the future, his life does not go unrecorded in the annals of Roman history. Funny thing, but I happen to have a copy of Josephus with me which I am taking to be rebound. Now Josephus was not a Christian, he was a Jew, living at the time of Christ, and the Emperor of Rome appointed him to write a history of Jews. Let me find the place—Ah—here it is:

'And there, arose about this time Jesus, a wise man, if indeed we should call him a man; for he was a doer of marvellous deeds, a teacher of men who receive the truth with pleasure. He won over many Jews and also many Greeks. This man was the Messiah. And when Pilate had condemned him to the Cross at the instigation of our own leaders, those who loved him from the first did not cease. For he appeared to them on the third day alive again, as the holy prophets had predicted and said many other wonderful things about him. And even now the race of Christians so named after him has not died out.'

Thinker: This is a most surprising statement from a pagan writer. Are there any others?

Curator: Well, Tacitus and Suetonius both refer to Jesus in their histories, while Pliny the younger describes early Christian belief in one of his letters. I will not bore you with any more facts. You see the life of Jesus Christ is by no means unsubstantiated. Excuse me, I must be passing along before the bookbinders closes.

(*Exit Curator*)

Thinker: Thank you so much for stopping. I had never realized before that Jesus Christ was as real an historical figure as Caesar, Napoleon or Churchill.

Voice: My friend, do not be content with that—Jesus Christ is not only a figure of history. He came not only to share the difficult life of men. He came for more than that.
(*Curtain opens on students*)

3rd Student: Well it's all been useless. What have we achieved? No one has listened to us though we've shouted, written and demonstrated.

1st Student: You're right—we've not even succeeded in making ourselves felt—let alone changed anything at all. The only way is action. We have said too much and acted too little. . . .

2nd Student: Something in the book I was reading about that . . . (*picks up book*) about sitting talking instead of doing . . . here it is, the Freedom Rock.

> Would you like to take a freedom walk
> When some don't care and the others mock
> And it's safer to sit at home and talk
> Than build the Freedom Rock.
>
> Do you want to march for freedom now
> Or wait ten years till they tell you how
> You've got to do more than they'll allow
> To sing the Freedom Rock.
>
> Are you scared to make that freedom run
> When someone out there is holding a gun
> And for all you know you may be the one
> Shot on the Freedom Rock.
>
> Black and white and yellow and red
> There's equal freedom when you're dead
> But some of us want it for the living instead
> Upon the Freedom Rock.
>
> We'll all be together on the final march
> And there's no turning back when the road gets harsh
> For this time there can't be a next time farce
> Or there'll be no Freedom Rock.

3rd Student: That's right—we need some action so dramatic, so decisive that the world will have to notice us.

1st Student: It might even cost us our lives.

3rd Student: What do you mean?
(*Students crowd together*)

3rd Student (*leaving group and sitting down*):   No, not that, anything else?

   (*Exit Students except 3rd student*)
         (*Song—'He was my brother . . .'*)
         (*Song ends with fade-up train*)
         (*Train fades into news report.*)
   (*Exit 3rd Student*)

Announcer: . . . spoke of the hopeful economic prospects for the coming decade. In Bedford this afternoon two people were killed when the northbound London–Newcastle express hit their car at a level crossing. It is believed that they were students, and posters on the vehicle suggested they were involved in a student demonstration. The driver of the train said that the car. . . .

Thinker: What tragic waste! Young men in the prime of their life with all their potentiality—thrown away for nothing. Life is too precious for this—what can the death of any man achieve?

Voice: Very little, my friend, unless it be the death of the Son of God.

Thinker: Oh, yes—we were talking before I was distracted—about why Jesus Christ came. Well, what was his great purpose?

Voice: For this cause I came into your world, that I might die the lowest death of humanity. . . .

Thinker: That I can never understand—a man who came to die.

Voice: Then look into the past if you would know the secret of the present.

   (*Time travel—Calvary background*)
   (*Enter Centurion*)

Centurion:

   What is it now? More trouble?
   Another Jew? I might have known it.
   These Jews, they buzz around the tail of trouble
   Like lascivious flies. Do they think we're here
   Because we love them? Is it their climate
   That holds us here? Why, think, Marcellus—
   By God, just dream of it. Today in Rome,
   Less than two thousand thirsty miles away,
   Fountains and squares and shadowed colonnades,

Men with smooth chins and girls who sometimes wash.
Well, who is it? . . . I see.
Another to be taken to that bone hill.
They're coming now. Just listen to them!—
My sword, Marcellus. I'll be back to dinner,
Unless this fellow is a reluctant dier
Who loves the world too well.

Halt! Stop that shouting. Why is he dressed like that?
His robes are purple. On his head
A hedge-crown. Where the thorns are driven
Berries of blood leap up . . . My orders differ.
Remove that crown—at once—return his clothes.
Kingship can wait until his throne is ready.
Till then, safe conduct. Hold your lines—
Especially that to windward: I've no fondness
For foreign spittle. Hold them. March . . .
Halt! Here's the place. Set down the cross.
You three attend to it. And remember, Marcus,
The blows are struck, the nails are driven
For Roman law and order.
Not for your private satisfaction.
Set to work.
(This grass is bare, sand-coloured: the hill
Quivers with heat.) What? As you please.
Seamless?—then dice for it. (The sun
Is brutal in this land, metallic.
It works for death, not life.) Well, is it done?
Now nail the board above: 'King of the Jews'.
That turns the mockery on them. Watch them wince
At the superscription. Look, their faces!
Hate. Which man is hated most,
Myself or him? He'll serve for both:
They know their limitations. They know,
Greek, Jew or Roman, there is one command,
One only. What's his name?—
He takes it quietly. From Nazareth?
I know it well. Who would exchange it
For this sad city, and become
The food of flies? Marcus there:
Give him some wine: he won't last long.

That strain of wrist, the arm's tension
And scarecrow hang of chest. Ah, well,
Poor devil, he's got decent eyes.
(*Change background to empty tomb*)

Voice: That awful death was not just to show that I cared, not just that I had entered your world. It was the very act by which man can know his Creator again in a personal, living relationship.

Thinker: But wasn't it defeat to die like that?

Voice: Look behind you and see the tomb in which that body lay—a tomb which could not contain the Son of God even for half a week. This is victory. Here in the history of your poor world is the event by which I set man free from ignorance of his Creator.

Thinker: You have bowed my mind with the sheer evidence, you have bowed my heart with the life of the Son of God, and now you ask me to bow my whole being before your throne, my God. I do not know which way to turn—and you people who have patiently watched our course toward the truth—you can help—we wish to know what you conclude. How seems the evidence to you? But as for me, I must decide, I must take time to think it out.

Chapter 7

Ideas for Community Service

The mass media have brought right into our drawing-rooms the dilemma of many senior citizens and other people in our society who are under-privileged or in need. The need constitutes a call to action. Much happiness and friendship can come to a group who engage in community service. There is fun in doing useful and interesting things. Here are some ideas:

1. Visiting the elderly

Many Welfare Departments are happy to hear of responsible young people who are prepared to visit the elderly and to do simple jobs and errands for them. This should be negotiated through an official department, as old people can rightly be suspicious of strangers knocking on doors, volunteering to help.

2. Decorating

Elderly people often live in old houses they cannot afford to redecorate. Under careful supervision, groups can bring great happiness to the occupants and a sense of achievement for themselves in this activity. Why not get the Church or group to pay for the materials? The leader should check that the work is completed to the occupier's satisfaction.

3. Gardening

Infirm, sick and elderly often cannot cope with their patch. This is obvious from looking over the fence. If you approach people carefully and sympathetically, not criticizing them, but suggesting that you recognize perhaps they could do with a little help, they will usually allow your group to go in and enjoy a tidying-up operation. Make sure someone in the group knows which are plants and which are weeds!

4. Clothing appeals

Many national and local philanthropic associations organize regular appeals. Help is usually invited in advertising the appeal by use of leaflet distribution. The centre needs staffing, clothes being bagged according to the type of items. Young men are useful in the evenings to stack the sacks.

5. 'Starvation Meals'

Why not organize a bread, cheese and water mid-day meal in a hall or open-air site where crowds congregate—and provide the meal? People will pay a reasonable price for these and all profits can be given to a charity which is concerned with feeding the hungry. If this meal is advertised in advance, many public-spirited people will be happy to participate. Make sure that those who share in the meal are given enough information about the project they are supporting. A display of posters, or a short filmstrip via back projection can gain further interest. A collecting box can be strategically placed.

6. Christmas meals for the elderly

This can involve a large group.

(a) Find out the need. Enquire of your local social welfare office or organize a survey of the district. (See appendix for further suggestions.)

(b) Make your project known to local traders. Very often they will give you reasonable discounts.

(c) Give plenty of advance notice of the event.

(d) Apportion various leaders, e.g. for buying and preparing food, cooking, laying tables, table decorations, entertaining, etc.

(e) Arrange transportation.

(f) Be sure that an adequate number of those who are organizing the meal sit down with the guests and share with them. This obviates the problem of the distinction between the 'do gooders' from the 'receivers', gives a sense of oneness and expresses a real desire and concern for the welfare of the whole person, not just for his stomach.

7. Outings

Coach outings for elderly and less mobile members of the community. Ensure enough transport with suitable drivers. Usually, old people don't like to be driven fast. Places of historic and local interest will bring enjoyment.

8. Baby sitting

It's not only the senior citizens who have problems. Many young couples cannot afford to pay baby-sitters and would love to have an evening out together. Organize a meal or social for young mums and dads and supply a baby-sitting service. Members of the fellowship or club should be given some initial basic training in child care. It can be helpful if baby-sitting is done in pairs. Make sure the sitters know where they can contact some responsible person in case of emergency.

9. Helping widows

Widows are sometimes the loneliest people in a community. Their husbands having done all the odd jobs around the house, they find many little things which need repairing—and have neither the tools nor the skill to do it. A careful approach by leaders of the group can often bring very grateful response from widows in need of help.

10. Care of church property

Gardens, graveyards, and church halls often need cleaning or refurbishing. Offers should be made to the local minister.

11. Entertaining overseas visitors

Many visitors and overseas students delight in an invitation to a home. Invite one or two to stay for the Christmas period and take time to entertain and share your country's way of life.

12. Local hospital radio

There are expanding opportunities for helpful contributions to programmes of local interest for hospital patients. Contact the local hospital secretary and enquire whether help is needed.

Chapter 8

Ideas for Fund Raising

Methods of fund raising have produced more than their share of heated debates at church meetings. What is essential is that, before adopting any method, we should be convinced in our own minds it is in no way unbiblical or unchristian.

This is not the place for an essay on Christian stewardship. There is much other excellent material which sets out the Biblical instruction about giving, but for the purpose of this section we feel we must stress these three important points:

(a) We are not concerned here with raising money for church funds. We are suggesting ways in which Christians can take the initiative in raising money for humanitarian and other good causes which are supported both by Christians and non-Christians.

(b) There is, we believe, a crucial difference between 'begging,' which we are not advocating, and the obtaining of a just reward for enterprise, initiative and the giving of a reasonable service.

(c) Where a church organization proposes to share in a fund-raising project of any kind, it should first make sure that it is acting with the approval of the church council or diaconate or of the appropriate church leaders.

The following ideas can usually be put into effect by a youth fellowship or club for the support of charitable causes:

1. A Stick-in for children

You will require wood off-cuts and glue. Set up your stick-in area where children can come, pay an entrance fee, and for an hour or two can stick blocks of all shapes and sizes together, making objects. Budding Picassos thrill at the opportunity! Make sure the child has an apron, and that adequate supervision is available at all times.

2. Stalls, etc.

Make a stall of sweets, cakes, candles—in fact of any saleable commodity which is attractive—and have a bazaar.

Side shows can sometimes be incorporated into a larger group project. For Bring and Buy Sales. Members and friends are invited to present goods for sale, and also to buy useful articles.

3. Car cleaning

For this you need a Church car park, or an area near to a public highway. Advertise clearly and widely the day and the timing of the event. All participants should be briefed about the care of vehicles. Use plastic buckets and suitable wash cloths. Work in teams of three or four, so that the car can be cleaned quickly—to the relief of the group organizers and also to the pleasure of the motorist. If you advertise a ten-minute car wash, make sure that you keep to time. Some practice on the leader's car can ensure efficiency and, we hope a very clean specimen.

4. Sponsored walks

Great care is required. If possible, the walk should be routed through country paths and quiet roads.

 (i) Make sure you have adequate marshalling for check points, which should be strategically placed en route and at crossing points.
 (ii) Each competitor should be given a sponsor form some days before the walk takes place. He seeks help from friends and neighbours, who sponsor him at so much a mile.
(iii) Transport should be available for any who can't last out the whole course, and refreshments should be obtainable at given points.
(iv) To get a large number of participants, contact local schools.
 (v) Young children should not be encouraged to take part in this activity.

152

5. Read-ins.

On the sponsorship principle, a 'read-in' can take place. Why not read the Bible through, day and night, over a weekend? Many other sponsorship ideas will come as a result of a brain-storming session with members of the youth group.

6. Clean-ins

Ask the leaders or sponsoring committees of the local community if you can undertake to conduct a spring-cleaning job on premises at a negotiated fee. As a club activity, this can not only raise cash, but stimulate comradeship. Careful supervision is essential. If the work entails any possbility of physical injury, you should take out insurance cover.

7. Non-stops

Sponsored non-stop games and activities generate a lot of local interest. There is literally no end to the possibilities. Some of the well-tried marathons have been table tennis, badminton, billiards, snooker, indoor football, pram-pushing, dart throwing, car tyre-rolling, canoeing, swimming, roller skating, cycling on rails indoors, reading and physical exercises.

8. Sponsorships galore

These need to be well advertised, organized and patronized. How about a silent sit-in (especially good for children!) or a sing-in with various local groups taking part? Those running out of songs are gradually eliminated as the time rolls on. A good musician is helpful. Spaghetti-eating is especially suitable for boys. (Or how about fasts?) These should be well supervised, especially if they last for any length of time. It is better for a group to go without one meal a day rather than trying to participate in a longer fast. Of course, the money they save on the meal goes to charity.

9. Opportunity knocks

Invite all local young people to provide items of entertainment for which suitable small prizes can be awarded. The audience can judge the entries by the length of their applause. Purchased programmes can be used as means of admission.

10. Miles of coins

These need careful organization and co-operation with the local constabulary. If it can be done on a public highway, so much the better, as passers-by are usually ready to help. The measured distance needs to be manned by the group and a time limit set. By means of posters, publicity and personal invitation people can be invited to join in this effort.

11. Novelties for fund raising

Combs, brushes, pencils, ball points and a host of other small items, each with group or company name stamped in gold, can be purchased fron numerous companies at a good discount and resold for the benefit of club events.

12. Re-making Christmas cards

Some groups print their own insert on white card stating that 'This is a re-make card for . . . charity'. Pictures from used cards are used to decorate the front. These can be attractively produced and are a lucrative means of raising cash.

13. Waste-paper collections

The growing shortage of raw materials for newsprint will increase the demand for the reprocessing of newspapers, etc. A reasonable price is paid for this commodity, and transport is provided. Usually a firm requires a minimum of two tons. You will need storage space, organized regular collections from your neighbourhood, and some muscle, but the rewards are attractive. Apart from time, there is no capital outlay if you have storage facilities. For information, see the yellow pages of local telephone directories.

14. Waste-material collection

Cloth, wool and metals in sufficient quantities can bring in reasonable returns to your exchequer. Organization is required, and publicity on a door-to-door pattern. Give clear information about the objects of the appeal. State when you are collecting—'We shall be in your area/road on the following dates . . .' Arrange transport, labour, a collecting centre and some semi-professional help in the sorting of metals. A large sledge-hammer is indispensable for condensing metal waste for storage and transport. The contents of sacks and bags of material should be clearly marked. String and carpet needles are a 'must' for sewing tops of sacks.

15. Marts

Local one-day secondhand furniture marts are a lucrative source of income. You need to plan months ahead! Your venue should be as near to a main street as possible. Advertise widely among friends and on a house-to-house plan. State clearly your object. Don't give the impression in your publicity that it is a jumble sale. Give a telephone number for people to ring with their offers, and make sure the 'phone is manned fully during the previous week. Take time to clean and polish furniture. On the day of sale allot a period for viewing. (If practicable, the whole of the previous day could be a viewing day.) Make sure of adequate staffing for stalls. Keep an eagle eye out for 'professional sharks' who want 'charity.' You are selling for charity, not giving charity at the sale! Do keep your takings in secure boxes and arrange for receipts to be given for all goods sold. If you can offer a transport service, state your price and terms. A set figure for journeys up to a certain distance saves time and is usually easier than 'so much a mile'. Some strong young men need to be organized for humping! Care must be taken in handling and transporting sold goods which should be clearly marked on labels (tied, not stuck) as to destination, etc.

More cash can be raised if a refreshment counter is organized throughout the day.

Often quite valuable antiques and goods are given for a good cause by well wishers. Do get these valued prior to the sale. In practice, we have found reputable dealers who have been extremely helpful not only in pricing but in assisting sales through their own outlets.

One prominent notice which is invaluable should be boldly displayed—'All goods are sold as seen. No guarantees are possible.'

16. Mart auctions

Similar arrangement as for Mart Sales, but you need some choice pieces and more valuable jewellery, etc., to attract the paying public. A catalogue should be made available and plenty of viewing time allotted. *It is essential to consult a qualified auctioneer before holding an auction. He will advise about terms of selling, and tell you how and by whom the sale should be conducted.*

17. Book fairs

All kinds of second-hand books and sets of quality magazines (e.g. *Homes and Gardens*, *National Geographic*) can be offered for sale.

A Committee should co-opt a book specialist to look over any collection before sale. A practised eye may find a valuable treasure.

Having decided on date, venue, times of opening, and the purpose to which all proceeds will be given, invite donors to bring books at appointed times or arrange for cars to pick them up from homes. This service is especially helpful to older donors, whose books may be a great asset but whose limited physical strength may discourage them from offering help.

The fair should be in the most public place available. A vacant shop, a market stall or a central hall should be the target. Car parking facilities are an important consideration. If parking is some distance from the fair, organize a team of young people with trolleys and offer a service to the customer.

Display is extremely important—try and give the impression of plenty of stock without overcrowding. A rule of thumb method of pricing would be 5p for paperbacks, 10p for hardbacks. Specially selected items should be priced by the 'specialist.' Over-pricing tends to cool sales. Remember that everything left over will have to be disposed of at the end of the fair.

A receipt for purchases is advisable, especially if the fair is on a large scale.

Refreshments served throughout the day can be another source of income and involvement.

Always make sure that all fund-raising events are conducted in circumstances of complete safety and under adequate supervision. 'Let all things be done decently and in an orderly fashion.' Always make public the amount of money raised, and the purpose to which it has been applied. After an event, the local press is always very willing to publicize the results. Alert them in good time and, if possible, get photographs of your effort to pass on to the local press—and pass them on quickly!

Finally, please read again the paragraphs at the beginning of this chapter!

Appendix A

Sources of Supply for Free Films

Names of organizations and addresses:

The Aluminium Development Association, 33 Grosvenor St., London, W.1.

Australian News and Information Bureau, Australia House, Strand, W.C.2.

Belgian Embassy, 103 Eaton Square, London, S.W.1.

British Electrical Development Association, 2 Savoy Hill, London, W.C.2.

British Iron and Steel Federation, Steel House, Tothill Street, London, S.W.1.

British Oxygen Co. Ltd., North Circular Road, Cricklewood, London, N.W.2.

British Transport Films, 25 Savile Row, London, W.1.

British Transport Film Library, Melbury House, Melbury Terrace, London NW1 6LP.

Central Film Library, Government Building, Bromyard Ave., London, W.3.

Richard Costain Ltd., 111 Westminster Bridge Road, London, S.E.1.

Concordia Films, Concordia House, 117/123 Golden Lane, London EC1Y 0TL.

Crookes Laboratories Ltd., Park Royal Road, London, N.W.10.

Don Summers Evangelistic Assoc., P.O. Box No. 4, Bristol BS99 7BR.

The G.B. Film Library, 1 Aintree Rd., Perivale, Greenford, Middx.

The Gas Council, Murdoch House, 1 Grosvenor Place, London, S.W.1.

Imperial Chemical Industries Ltd., Imperial Chemical House, Millbank, London, S.W.1.

Information Service of India, High Commission of India, India House, Aldwych, London, W.C.2.

International Wool Secretariat, Dorland House, 18–20 Regent St., London, W.1.

Irish Tourist Office, 71 Regent St., London, W.1.

Japan National Tourist Organization, 167 Regent St., London W.1.

National Coal Board Film Library, Hobart House, 2 Grosvenor Place, London, S.W.1.

New Zealand Films, New Zealand House, Haymarket, London, S.W.1.

National Film Board of Canada, Canada House Library, 3 Grosvenor Square, London, W.1.

The Nuffield Organization, The Film Librarian, B.M.C. Films Section, Cowley, Oxford.

Petroleum Films Bureau, 4 Brook St., London W1Y 2AY.

Rank Film Library, Rank Audio Visual Ltd., P.O. Box 70, Great West Road, Brentford, Middx.

Royal Norwegian Embassy, 25 Belgrave Square, London, S.W.1.

Scottish Central Film Library, 16/17 Woodside Terrace, Charing Cross, Glasgow, C.3.

Shell-Mex and B.P. Film Library, 25 The Burroughs, Hendon, London, N.W.4.

Sound Services Ltd., Wilton Crescent, Merton Park, London, S.W.19.

Unilever Ltd., Unilever House, Blackfriars, London, E.C.4.

United Film Services, 13 King St., Leicester, LE1 6RN (entertainment films).

World Wide Films, Shirley House, 27 Camden Road, London N.W.1.

Zionist Federation, 77 Gt. Russell Street, London, W.C.1.

Most tourist (national) organizations have films which are available.

Appendix B

Ideas for Celebrating Christmas

A.   A Christmas Carol. Traditional songs of a simple character have been sung since the fifteenth century.

B. Christmas Tree. Originated in Germany, though many countries also claim that this tradition belongs to them.

C. Christmas Card. Mr. William Dobson of Birmingham, England, designed a card to cheer a friend in 1844. The following year he sent many lithographic copies to his friends. From there the idea spread rapidly.

D. Christmas Gift. Tradition says the original Santa Claus was a certain Nicholas, a wealthy bishop of Myra in Asia Minor. The custom of giving to children is believed to have begun with him, though the whole essence of the Christmas message (John 3: 16) is embraced in the idea of giving.

Apply to libraries for books on traditions and customs.

E. Christian Giving to charities. Charities such as TEAR Fund, 39 Draycott Place, London S.W.1, and Christian Aid, 2 Sloane Square, London, S.W.1, often supply excellent material for Christmas, including carol sheets, and are always glad to receive offerings for relief of those in need.

Appendix C

London Underground and Railway Stations

(See page 73)

1.	Oval	13.	Liverpool Street
2.	Blackfriars	14.	Waterloo
3.	Baker Street	15.	Barking
4.	Swiss Cottage	16.	Lancaster Gate
5.	Park Royal	17.	Stratford
6.	St. John's Wood	18.	Queensway
7.	Warren Street	19.	Bank
8.	Tower Hill	20.	Mile End
9.	Redbridge	21.	Turnham Green
10.	Victoria	22.	Shoreditch
11.	Parsons Green	23.	Gunnersbury
12.	Gospel Oak	24.	Turnpike Lane

538